D1434471

CYBERTYPES

Race, Ethnicity, and Identity
on the Internet

CYBERTYPES

Race, Ethnicity, and Identity on the Internet

LISA NAKAMURA

ROUTLEDGE
New York and London

Published in 2002 by
Routledge
29 West 35th Street
New York, NY 10001

Published in Great Britain by
Routledge
11 New Fetter Lane
London EC4P 4EE

10 9 8 7 6 5 4 3 2 1

The publisher and the author are grateful for permission to reprint the following: Portions of chapter 1 appear as "After/Images of Identity: Gender, Technology, and Identity Politics" in *Reload: Rethinking Women and Culture*, edited
by Austin Booth and Mary Flanagan, MIT Press, forthcoming. Portions of chapter 2 appeared as "Race In/For Cyberspace: Textual Performance and Racial
Passing on the Internet" in *Works and Days* 25/26 (Fall 1995/Winter 1996).
Portions of chapter 2 appeared as "Head-Hunting in Cyberspace: Identity
Tourism, Asian (?) Avatars, and Racial Passing in Web-Based Chatspaces," in
The Women's Review of Books, February 2001. Portions of chapter 3 appear as
"Race in the Construct, or the Construction of Race: New Media and Old Iden-
tities in *The Matrix*" in *Domain Errors! A Cyberfeminist Handbook of Tactics*,
edited by Michelle Wright, Maria Fernandez, and Faith Wilding, Autonomedia
Press, forthcoming. A slightly different version of chapter 4 was originally pub-
lished in *Race in Cyberspace*, edited by Beth E. Kolko, Lisa Nakamura, and
Gilbert B. Rodman, copyright 2000, Routledge. Portions of chapter 5 appeared
as "Race" in *Unspun: Key Terms for the World Wide Web and Culture*, edited by
Thomas Swiss, copyright 2001, New York University Press, 2001.

Library of Congress Cataloging-in-Publication Data

Nakamura, Lisa.
    Cybertypes : race, ethnicity, and identity on the Internet / Lisa Nakamura.
        p. cm.
    Includes bibliographical references and index.
    ISBN 0-415-93836-8 — ISBN 0-415-93837-6 (pbk.)
    1. Race awareness. 2. Race discrimination. 3. Internet—Social aspects. 4.
Cyberspace—Social aspects. I. Title.

HT1523 .N35 2002
305.8'00285'4678—dc21   2001048945

CONTENTS

ACKNOWLEDGMENTS

I would like to thank Sonoma State University's English Department and the School of Arts and Humanities for travel funding to conferences, research support, and days released from teaching to attend professional events. Kathy Charmaz, Elaine McHugh, Richard Senghas, Adam Hill, and Dorothy Friedel of the Sonoma State Faculty Writing Group and Scott Miller, Tim Wandling, Anne Goldman, Leilani Nishime, and Kim Hester-Williams of the Sonoma State University Cultural Studies Group read and commented upon almost every word of this book. Leilani Nishime and Kim Hester-Williams deserve extra special thanks for being my academic sisters and the best beta testers in the world for wacky ideas. (If it weren't for that Chinese lunch we had together last summer, my concluding chapter would not exist!) Scott Miller and Tim Wandling were and continue to be tremendously supportive and generous friends and colleagues, and I thank them both for the errands run, advice given, and long downloads in our offices at SSU.

I would also like to thank my research assistants at Sonoma State: Drea Moore, Dean Klotz, Rebecca Small, and Jamie Balangue. Amelia Shapiro and Rosene Gubele provided invaluable assistance which supported this research as well. Back in the early days when I was afraid of computers, Greg Haun and Jay Beale explained how the Internet works and deserve much thanks for their patience. Alena Nahabedian and Daniel Thomas gave me some great lessons in postmodern subjectivity and much-needed tolerance on the domestic front. Barbara Guetti, my thesis director at Reed, was my first model of the "life of the mind." Fred Kaplan, Jane Marcus, and Mary Ann Caws are all patient, exemplary teachers and admirable people who have been models of responsible scholarship.

Much love to the San Francisco Ladies' Reading Group: Christina Boufis, Laura Mann, Tina Olsen, Victoria Olsen, and Susie Wise. I can't think of a greater group of women with whom to share issues, and everything I know about being a lady I learned from them.

David Silver, Greta Niu, Tara McPherson, T. V. Reed, Randy

Bass, Wahneema Lubiano, and Alondra Nelson provided expert and inspiring manuscript review, commentary on conference papers, and talks which generated much of the thinking in this book. Also thanks to my generous and supportive colleagues in Norway: Espen Aarseth of the University of Bergen and Tore Slaata of the University of Oslo.

Mark Poster of University of California, Irvine and Donna Haraway of University of California, Santa Cruz deserve an immense amount of thanks; their innovative, groundbreaking scholarship literally made many of these ideas possible, and critical cybercultures studies as a discipline could not exist without it, leaving this book without a shelf to sit on. Though I was never their student or colleague, they provided cyber-mentorship and the kind of encouragement that a young scholar hopes to come across once in a lifetime. I began to believe that I could write a book on race and cyberspace and that people might want to read it because of their kind words early on. Mark and Donna's generosity was of the purest sort, since there was nothing in it for them at all but additional work. I am most grateful to them for their assistance and support.

Amelie Hastie is simply the best, most brilliant, and kindest friend in the world. She has been a patient counselor (without her, chapter 2 would not exist), a tireless mentor (despite being younger than me), and a great reviewer of the work. She turned me on to Dean MacCannell's *The Tourist*, and continues to give me great guidance, support, and advice.

My parents, especially my father, David Nakamura, always made sure that I had good computer equipment and every other kind of support. My 99-year-old poet grandmother Nellie Nakamura gave me expensive books when I was a child and encouraged the love of reading and literature. David K. Nakamura, my brother, deserves props for explaining how sound technology such as digital remastering works and for sharing his knowledge of Japanese pop culture. My sister Judy Nakamura is an expert on Asian-American popular culture and generously kept me supplied with website URL's, "You Know You're Japanese American If" e-mails, and other vital bits of research. (She's not internationally known, but she's known to rock the microphone.)

Matthew Byrnie at Routledge and Thomas Foster of Indiana

University are responsible for most of the improvements made to this text in its transformation from a draft to a book. They both worked astonishingly quickly to expedite its production. Matt is the James Brown of academic publishing—he is beyond a doubt the hardest working man in the business, as well as the smartest. He displayed amazing aptitude for working with a very pregnant author, and has helped to break me of some of my most egregious writing tics. This book would not exist without him. Tom is my ideal reviewer, and a person whose critical judgment I trust absolutely. This would be a better book had I been able to implement all of his astute suggestions.

To my beautiful daughter Laura Emiko Burns, for arriving a week before the completion of this book, as well as being the inspiration for some of its concepts and ideas. You have made my life so wonderful! And to my husband, Martin Burns, for being the very best supporter, for having more faith in me than I had in myself, and for helping me to handle the logistics of everyday life and putting up with my sometimes trying ways. I admire his talents every day and feel very privileged that I get to benefit from them on such a regular basis. He always believed I could do this work and he deserves the most thanks of all.

INTRODUCTION

The Internet is a place where race happens. In the early days of the Net, technological visionaries imagined the online world as a utopian space where everything—even transcending racism—was possible. But now the Internet "revolution" is over, a fact upon which nearly everyone, from hackers to academics to dot-com investors, agrees. This book looks at what happened to race when it went online, and how our ideas about race, ethnicity, and identity continue to be shaped and reshaped every time we log on, even if we've just entered the post-Internet "epoch."[1]

After years of idealistic technohype, David Brooks wrote, in the *New York Times Magazine*,

> It's goodbye to the epoch—which must have lasted all of seven years—in which people chatted excitedly about free-agent nations, distance being dead, I.P.O.'s, the long boom and those dot-com ads during the Super Bowl that showed global children united by the wonders of instant communication. One minute you've got zip-drive techies pulling all-nighters amid their look-at-me-I'm-wacky workstations, and the next moment—poof—it seems so stale. Suddenly, it doesn't really matter much if the speed of microprocessors doubles with the square root of every lunar eclipse (or whatever Moore's law was). And so just like a used-bong sale in 1978 or a yellow-tie auction in 1990, scenes like this [. . .] bring a psychological decade to a sobering close. What started out as the biggest revolution since Gutenberg ends up as a giant yard sale [. . .]. What's gone is the sense that the people who are using the stuff are on the cutting edge of history and everyone else is roadkill. (28)

I started the research that led to this book in 1995, a year after Brooks dates the beginning of the Internet epoch, and completed it in 2001, the year he and most pundits agree brought the end of the Internet's heyday. At three years shy of a decade, it's a short-lived epoch indeed. Perhaps it succumbed to "Internet time," that compression of time to which we've grown accustomed in our high-tech lives.[2]

In these post-Internet times, it may be true that possessing access to the Internet no longer guarantees one a place at the "cutting edge of history." However, *lack of access* to the Internet—often found along raced, classed, and still, to a narrowing extent, gendered lines—continues to cut particular bodies *out* of various histories in the making. The epochal terms used by Brooks to describe the end of the "new economy" are characteristic of much popular intellectual writing on the Internet: those people who were run over, routed around, or simply denied access to the Internet are characterized as "roadkill" on the information superhighway.[3] This online roadkill is, quite simply, the poor and people of color.

Though Brooks writes that in 2001 there is no longer the sense that Internet nonusers are roadkill (a debatable claim indeed, considering recent concern over the "digital divide" that separates technology haves from have-nots), he does acknowledge that it was once thought so during those crucial years in which the discursive landscape of the Internet was being formed. Hence, people of color were functionally absent from the Internet at precisely that time when its discourse was acquiring its distinctive contours.

The repercussions of the discursive gap are immense, for, as I stated earlier, the Internet is a place where race happens; even in the absence of users of color, images of race and racialism proliferate in cyberspace. The ideological uses to which race is put in this medium must be examined before we can even begin to consider cyberspace's promise as a democratic and progressive medium. Daniel Punday is one of many cyberculture scholars who pose the question, Can the Internet propagate genuinely new and nonracist (and nonsexist and nonclassist) ways of being, or does it merely reflect our culture at large? Punday identifies two phases of Internet scholarship, the first and most utopian of which asserts that the former is true while the second asserts the latter. He writes that "quite contrary to the early belief that cyberspace offers a way to escape gender, race, and class as conditions of social interaction [. . .] recent critics suggest that online discourse is woven of stereotypical cultural narratives that reinstall precisely those conditions" (199).[4] In this passage, he claims that this second phase of scholarship has be-

come the dominant one: "these critics are debating whether participants in online discourse are constructing coherent identities that
shed light on the real world or whether they are merely tacking together an identity from media sources. As critics have gradually begun to accept the latter, they have lost confidence in the socially
transformative possibilities of online discourse" (204).

There is no doubt that the Internet is a "socially transformative"
force; what seems to be at issue here is rather the specific nature of
that ongoing transformation as well as its particular object. Rather
than adopting a utopian or pessimistic view in which the Internet is
viewed as either a vector for progressive change in the classical liberal tradition or as the purveyor of crude and simplistic "stereotypical cultural narratives," it seems crucial to first narrow the focus a
bit and examine the specific means by which identities are deployed
in cyberspace. Currently, "popular attitudes toward the Internet
tend to be maddeningly bipolar—either the Net changes everything
or the Net changes nothing" (Heilemann 138). Of course, the truth
lies between these two poles: the Net changes *some* things. Images
of race on the Net are both "stereotyped" at times, as in some chat
rooms, cyberpunk fictions, and advertisements, and at other times,
race is deployed in creative coalition building that creates a sense of
community and racial identity online. As scholars become more
sensitized to issues of diversity online,[5] there is a welcome shift in
emphasis from simply recognizing that racial inequity does exist
there to a growing concern with how race is represented in cyberspace, for the Internet is above all a discursive and rhetorical space,
a place where "race" is created as an effect of the net's distinctive
uses of language. Hence, it is crucial to examine not only the wide
variety of rhetorical conditions of utterance, reception, audience,
and user/speaker that create particular communicative situations in
cyberspace, but also to trace the ways in which this array of situations creates "cybertypes," or images of racial identity engendered
by this new medium. Only then will it be possible to assess the Net's
potential for "social transformation."

What ideological and cultural work does race do in cyberspace?
The question demands a number of different types of critical approaches and examples, since cyberspace makes so many different
kinds of narrative possible: user-to-user narratives (such as those

produced in chat rooms or e-mail) and user-to-interface narratives (that is to say, what happens when users encounter design issues and interact with them) constitute just two examples. There is also a formidable array of narratives about cyberspace, such as cyberpunk fictions and popular advertisements for the Internet, that inform the ways that users envision and interact with its racial terrain. Each chapter of this book addresses the question of racial cybertyping's operations (for better or worse) in the different rhetorical spaces of and around the Internet in an attempt to acknowledge their variety and particularity, for it makes no more sense to discuss the Net as one "thing" than it does to discuss literature without reference to period, genre, style, or audience.

Chapter 1, "Cybertyping and the Work of Race in the Age of Digital Reproduction," examines the ways that race gets coded for different kinds of work in the information economy, and traces the ways that cybertyping proliferates as part of a cultural matrix that surrounds the Internet. While foreign workers are often glorified as exemplary information workers (as in the case of immigrant Asian engineers with H1B visas), American racial minorities, in particular African Americans, are troped quite differently, as outsiders to digital economies and systems of representation. This permits a kind of cosmetic cosmopolitanism that perpetuates a digital divide that splits along the axis of racial representations as well as along patterns of computer access organized around racial difference. Racism in this country is ignored in favor of celebrating the diversity of "foreign" information workers, who are represented in advertisements as a Benetton-like rainbow of racial difference—decorative, exotic, and comfortably distant.

Chapter 2, entitled "Head-Hunting on the Internet: Identity Tourism, Avatars, and Racial Passing in Textual and Graphical Chat Spaces," focuses on user-to-user interactions in social role-playing spaces online. While these spaces could be categorized as "games," the MUDs, MOOs, and chat rooms that I examine,[6] specifically LambdaMOO and Club Connect, are also theatrical and discursive spaces where identity is performed, swapped, bought, and sold in both textual and graphic media. When users create characters to deploy in these spaces, they are electing to perform versions of themselves as raced and gendered beings. When users' characters, or "avatars," are differently raced from the user, the opportunity for online recreational passing or "identity tourism" arises; that is to say, users perform stereotyped versions of the "Oriental" that perpetuate old mythologies about racial difference. And as Caren Kaplan points out in *Questions of Travel*, tourists operate from a position of privilege and entitlement (62); to be a tourist is to possess mobility, access, and the capital to satisfy curiosities about "native" life. Chat-space participants who take on identities as samurai and geisha constitute the darker side of postmodern identity, since the "fluid selves" they create (and often so lauded by postmodern theorists) are done so in the most regressive and stereotyped of ways. These kinds of racial identity plays stand as a critique of the notion of the digital citizen as an ideal cogito whose subjectivity is liberated by cyberspace. On the contrary, only too often does one person's "liberation" constitute another's recontainment within the realm of racialized discourse. The socially marginalized have a different relation to postmodernity than do members of majority cultures or races. Hence, they have a different relation to cyberspace, or to put it another way, they "do" virtuality differently. That is to say, the type of fragmentation of self or subjectivity they experience online (and as decentered subjects in postmodern culture) differs from that of "majority" users. Though Phillip Brian Harper doesn't look at the Internet specifically in *Framing the Margins: The Social Logic of Postmodern Culture*, he does cite technology as one of the forces engendering the fragmentation characteristic of life in postmodern times, and asserts that "what 'minority' subjects often experience as their primary source of disorientation—the social effects of their difference in contexts where it is construed as negative—will complicate their experience of what has heretofore been conceived as the 'general' disorientation characteristic of the postmodern condition" (29). In other words, being raced is in itself a disorienting position. Being raced in cyberspace is doubly disorienting, creating multiple layers of identity construction. While on the one hand people of color have always been postmodern (and by extension "virtual"), if postmodernism is defined as that way of seeing subjectivity as decentered, fragmented, and marginalized, on the other hand their lack of access to technology and popular figuration as the "primitive" both on- and offline (those virtual samurai and geisha are certainly not to be found in "modern," let alone post-modern, Japan) positions them simultaneously in the nostalgic world of the premodern. The Internet is certainly a place where social differences such as race are frequently construed as negative. While everyone in cyberspace is disoriented, people of color in cyberspace come to the medium already in this state, already marginalized, fragmented, and imbricated within systems of signification that frame them in multiple and often contradictory ways. The celebration of the "fluid self" that simultaneously lauds postmodernity as a potentially liberatory sort of worldview tends to overlook the more disturbing aspects of the fluid, marginalized selves that already exist offline in the form of actual marginalized peoples, which is not nearly so romantic a formulation. But then, this is symptomatic of both postmodern theory and cyberculture studies, neither of which wants to look at race critically. As Harper claims, "the experiences of socially marginalized groups implicitly inform the 'general' postmodern condition without being accounted for in theorizations of it" (4). Indeed, if we are all marginalized and decentered, or if we are all equally "virtual" when we are in cyberspace, what need is there to refer to race at all in discussions of identity online or in a postmodern world?

But, of course, we are not all equally on the margins in the world offline, just as we are not all equally "virtual" in relation to the Internet. And as our culture's investment in computer gaming such as chat rooms and interactive social spaces only continues to grow, it becomes all the more important that we focus a critical gaze on the ways that race is played in these theaters of identity.

While chapter 2 identifies cybertyped versions of race enacted by users in both graphical and textual chat spaces, chapter 3, entitled "Race in the Construct and the Construction of Race: The 'Consensual Hallucination' of Multiculturalism in the Fictions of Cyberspace," examines the source of these "types" in popular narratives about cyberspace. The study of racial impersonation and passing on MOOs and MUDs reveals a great deal about how people "do" race online; this chapter locates the origin of some of these master narratives about how race is done online in 1980s and '90s cyberpunk narratives. Close readings of four influential cyberpunk texts—two from the 1980s (Ridley Scott's film *Blade Runner* and

William Gibson's novel *Neuromancer*) and two from the 1990s, (Neal Stephenson's novel *Snow Crash* and Andy and Larry Wachowski's film *The Matrix*)—reveal the ways that cyberspace is racialized in popular narratives, and identify a progression from relatively simple and traditional forms of techno-orientalism to a more nuanced vision of racial hybridity which nonetheless performs its own variety of cybertyping.

Chapter 4, "'Where Do You Want to Go Today?': Cybernetic Tourism, the Internet, and Transnationality," picks up where chapter 3 leaves off by extending the range of inquiry to television and print advertisements produced by large telephony and networking companies like IBM, Compaq, MCI, and Microsoft. These advertisements, which appeared in mainstream and academic publications, are symptomatic of the ways that corporate discourse cybertypes use race as a visual commodity for the user. Images of exotic travel in the "third world," and "primitive" places and people, are part of a persistent pattern of signification that reinforces the notion of the Western computer and network user as a tourist in cyberspace. Earlier colonial discourses that privilege the Western gaze and the sense of freedom, expansiveness, and mastery engendered by its deployment are directly referenced in the quasi-anthropological visual language of these ads, which often evoke images from *National Geographic* magazines of days gone by.

Chapter 5, "Menu-Driven Identities: Making Race Happen Online," examines the relationship between the user and the interface, in particular those interfaces on the Internet such as website portals and e-mail programs, which most users encounter on a daily basis, and traces the ways that interface design can produce cybertyped versions of race. When interfaces present us with menus that insist on a limited range of choices vis-à-vis race, this discursive narrowing of the field of representation can work to deny the existence of ways of being raced that don't fit into neatly categorizable boxes. Registration pages on websites that demand that users click a box describing them as "Asian," "African American," or "Hispanic" create a textual environment in which mixtures of or variations on these already contested categories are literally impossible to express using this interface. This kind of menu-driven racial identity not only denies the possibility of a mestiza consciousness at a time when our social realities are bending to acknowledge the existence of various forms of racial and cultural hybridity, but also serves a racist ideology which benefits from retaining solid and simplistic notions of race. I juxtapose this reading of corporate interfaces that cybertype users in limiting and simplistic ways to another example, that of ethnic identity e-mail jokes that circulate between groups of users who can share a more fluid, less essentialized sense of racial identity. As John Heilemann notes,

> Andy Grove, C.E.O. of Intel, asserted in a 2001 interview with *Wired* that Internet penetration in the U.S. is substantially ahead of the rest of the world. In the next five years, one thing that is likely to happen is that Internet penetration in the rest of the world is going to replicate what's happened here. And that is going to let—Seattle-style protests notwithstanding—a globalization of culture, of business, of communications achieve a level of pervasiveness that in itself will change the world significantly. (139)

Grove is speaking from the point of view of a person who's been involved in the Internet's infrastructure and commerce from the beginning, not as a scholar of critical theory, ethnic studies, or progressive politics. And in that sense he is typical of most of the captains of the Internet industry machine: his view is that "globalization of culture, of business, of communications" is an unambiguously good thing. Phallic metaphors of the Internet as a peculiarly "penetrative" medium sound patriarchal, as indeed they are. But more to the point, they figure globalization as the result of that penetration, a penetration that cannot be resisted, despite "Seattle-style protests." Clearly, there is a great deal at stake here. In *The Souls of Black Folk*, W. E. B. Du Bois writes that "the problem of the Twentieth Century is the problem of the color-line" (v). At the end of the Internet epoch and the advent of the twenty-first century, this is *still* the problem that haunts cyberspace. It is crucial that scholarly inquiry examine the ways that racism is perpetuated by both globalization and communications technologies like the Internet across a range of discursive fields and cultural matrices. This becomes all the more important as locales outside of the United

States submit to "penetration" by the medium, and consequently undergo the sometimes-wrenching transformations that accompany such discursive shifts. This book examines the ways that race is configured in English-language based cyberspaces hosted in the United States. However, in the face of Grove's vision of Internet-driven globalization (which there is no reason in my mind to doubt) it is clear that more research needs to be done on the emerging terrain of race, ethnicity, and racism in non-American cyberspaces. America is not the only place where "digital divides" separate the "roadkill" from the digerati.

< 1 >

CYBERTYPING AND THE WORK OF RACE IN THE AGE OF DIGITAL REPRODUCTION

Software engineers and academics have something in common: they both like to make up new words. And despite the popular press's glee in mocking both computer-geek and academic jargon, there are several good arguments to be made for the creation of useful neologisms, especially in cases where one of these fields of study is brought to bear on the other. The Internet has spawned a whole new set of vocabulary and specialized terminology because it is a new tool for communicating that has enabled a genuinely new discursive field, a way of generating and consuming language and signs that is distinctively different from other, older media. It is an example of what is dubbed "the new media" (a term refreshingly different from the all-purpose *post-* prefix so familiar to critical theorists, but destined to date just as badly). Terms such as *cybersex, online, file compression, hypertext link,* and *downloading* are now part of the Internet user's everyday vocabulary since they describe practices or virtual objects that lack analogues in either offline life or other media. The new modes of discourse enabled by the Internet require new descriptive terminologies and conceptual frameworks.

Just as engineers and programmers routinely come up with neologisms to describe new technologies, so too do academics and cultural theorists coin new phrases and terms to describe concepts they wish to introduce to the critical conversation. While these attempts are not always well advised, and certainly do contribute at times to the impenetrable and unnecessarily confusing nature of high theory's rhetoric, there are some compelling reasons that this move seems peculiarly appropriate in the case of academic studies of the

Internet. Lev Manovich and Espen Aarseth both make a persuasive case for the creation and deployment of a distinctively new set of terminologies to describe the new media, in particular the Internet. In *The Language of New Media* Manovich asserts that "comparing new media to print, photography, or television will never tell us the whole story" and that "to understand the logic of new media we need to turn to computer science. It is there that we may expect to find the new terms, categories, and operations which characterize media which became programmable. From media studies, we move to something which can be called software studies; from media theory—to software theory" (65). This statement calls for a radical shift in focus from traditional ways of envisioning media to a new method that takes the indispensability of the computer-machine into account. It truly does call for a reconceptualization of media studies, and constitutes a call for new terms more appropriate to "software studies" to best convey the distinctive features of new media, in particular the use of the computer.

Manovich identifies two "layers" to new media: the cultural layer, which is roughly analogous to "content," and the computer layer, or infrastructure, interface, or other machine-based forms that structure the computer environment. His argument that the computer layer can be expected to have a "significant influence on the cultural logic of media" (63) is in some sense not original; the notion that form influences content (and vice versa) has been around since the early days of literary criticism. It has been conceded for some time now that certain forms allow or disallow the articulation of certain ideas. However, what is original about this argument is its claim that our culture is becoming "computerized" in a wholesale and presumably irrevocable fashion. This is a distinctively different proposition from asserting the importance of, say, electronic *literacy*, a paradigm that is still anchored by its terminology in the world of a very old medium: writing. Manovich calls for a new terminology, native to the computer; he goes on to write that

in new media lingo, to "transcode" something is to translate it into another format. The computerization of culture gradually accomplishes similar transcoding in relation to all cultural categories and concepts. That is, cultural categories and concepts are substituted, on the level of meaning and/or language, by new ones which derive from the computer's ontology, epistemology, pragmatics. New media thus acts as a forerunner of this more general process of cultural re-conceptualization. (64)

If we follow this proposition, we can see that our culture is in the process of being "transcoded" by the computer's "ontology, epistemology, pragmatics." While this statement has far-reaching implications, at the least it can be seen as an argument for a new openness in new media studies toward the adoption of a terminology that at least acknowledges the indispensable nature of the computer in the study of new media. This would be a transcoded kind of terminology, one that borrows from the language of the computer itself rather than from the language of critical theory or old media studies. In his article "The Field of Humanistic Informatics and its Relation to the Humanities," Espen Aarseth argues that the study of new media needs to be a "separate, autonomous field, where the historical, aesthetic, cultural and discursive aspects of the digitalization of our society may be examined [. . .]. We cannot leave this new development to existing fields, because they will always privilege their traditional methods, which are based on their own empirical objects" (n.p.).

In an attempt to transcode the language of race and racialism that I observed online, I coined the term *cybertype* to describe the distinctive ways that the Internet propagates, disseminates, and commodifies images of race and racism. The study of racial cybertypes brings together the cultural layer and the computer layer; that is to say, cybertyping is the process by which computer/human interfaces, the dynamics and economics of access, and the means by which users are able to express themselves online interacts with the "cultural layer" or ideologies regarding race that they bring with them into cyberspace. Manovich is correct in asserting that we must take into account the ways that the computer determines how ideological constructs such as race get articulated in this new medium.

Critical theory itself is a technology or machine that produces a particular kind of discourse, and I'd like to conduct a discursive experiment by poaching a term from nineteenth-century print technology. That term is *stereotype*.

The word *stereotype* is itself an example of machine language, albeit a precomputer machine language; the first stereotype was a mechanical device that could reproduce images relatively cheaply, quickly, and in mass quantities. Now that computer-enabled image-reproducing technology like the Internet is faster, cheaper, and more efficient than ever before, how does that machine language translate into critical terms? Might we call new formulations of machine-linked identity *cybertypes*? This is a clunky term; in hacker-speak it would be called a "kludge" or "hack" because it's an improvised, spontaneous, seat-of-the-pants way of getting something done. (Critical theory, like the software industry, is a machine that is good at manufacturing linguistic kludges and hacks). I'd like to introduce it, however, because it acknowledges that identity online is still *typed*, still mired in oppressive roles even if the body has been left behind or bracketed.[1] I pose it as a corrective to the disturbingly utopian strain I see embodied in most commercial representations of the Internet in general. Chosen identities enabled by technology, such as online avatars, cosmetic and transgender surgery and body modifications, and other cyberprostheses are not breaking the mold of unitary identity but rather shifting identity into the realm of the "virtual," a place not without its own laws and hierarchies. Supposedly "fluid" selves are no less subject to cultural hegemonies, rules of conduct, and regulating cultural norms than are "solid."

While telecommunications and medical technologies can challenge some gender and racial stereotypes, they can produce and reflect them as well. Cybertypes of the biotechnologically enhanced or perfected woman and of the Internet's invisible minorities, who can log on to the Net and be taken for "white," participate in an ideology of liberation from marginalized and devalued bodies. This kind of technology's greatest promise to us is to eradicate otherness—to create a kind of better living through chemistry, so to speak. Images of science freeing women from their aging bodies, which make it more difficult to conceive children and ward off cellulite, freeing men from the curse of hair loss, and freeing minorities online from the stigma of their race (since no one can see them), reinforce a "postbody" ideology that reproduces the assumptions of the old one. In an example of linguistic retrofitting, I've termed this phenomenon an example of the "meet the new boss, same as the old boss" product line). In other words, machines that offer identity prostheses to redress the burdens of physical "handicaps" such as age, gender, and race produce cybertypes that look remarkably like racial and gender stereotypes. My research on cross-racial impersonation in an online community, described in chapter 2, reveals that when users are free to choose their own race, all were assumed to be white. And many of those who adopted nonwhite personae turned out to be white male users masquerading as exotic samurai and horny geishas.

Of course, this kind of vertiginous identity play, which produces and reveals cybertyping, is not the fault of or even primarily an effect of technology. Microsoft's advertising slogan, "Where do you want to go today?" is another example of the discourse of technological liberation, and it situates the agency directly where it belongs: with the user. Though computer memory modules double in speed every couple of years, users are still running operating systems that reflect phantasmatic visions of race and gender. Moore's Law, which states that computer processing speeds double every eighteen months, does not obtain in the "cultural layer." In the end, despite academic and commercial discourses, to the contrary it does come down to bodies—bodies with or without access to the Internet, telecommunications, and computers and the cultural capital necessary to use them; bodies with or without access to basic healthcare, let alone high-tech pharmaceuticals or expensive forms of elective surgery.

Cybertypes are more than just racial stereotypes "ported" to a new medium. Because the Internet is interactive and collectively authored, cybertypes are created in a peculiarly collaborative way; they reflect the ways that machine-enabled interactivity gives rise to images of race that both stem from a common cultural logic and seek to redress anxieties about the ways that computer-enabled communication can challenge these old logics. They perform a crucial role in the signifying practice of cyberspace; they stabilize a sense of a white self and identity that is threatened by the radical fluidity and disconnect between mind and body that is celebrated in so much cyberpunk fiction. Bodies get tricky in cyberspace; that sense of dis-embodiment that is both freeing and disorienting creates a profound malaise in the user that stable images of race work to fix in place.

Cybertypes are the images of race that arise when the fears, anx-ieties, and desires of privileged Western users (the majority of Inter-net users and content producers are still from the Western nations) are scripted into a textual/graphical environment that is in constant flux and revision. As Rey Chow writes in "Where Have All the Na-tives Gone?" images of raced others become necessary symptoms of the postcolonial condition. She writes that "the production of the native is in part the production of our postcolonial modernity" (30), and that "we see that in our fascination with the 'authentic native' we are actually engaged in a search for the aura even while our search processes themselves take us farther and farther from that 'original' point of identification" (46). The Internet is certainly a postcolonial discursive practice, originating as it does from both scientific discourses of progress and the Western global capitalistic project. When Chow attributes our need for stabilizing images of the "authentic native" to the "search for the aura," or original and authentic object, she is transcoding Walter Benjamin's formulation from "The Work of Art in the Age of Mechanical Reproduction" into a new paradigm. In a subsection to her essay entitled "The Na-tive in the Age of Discursive Reproduction," Chow clarifies her use of Benjamin to talk about postcolonialism and the function of the "native." While Benjamin maintained that technology had radically changed the nature of art by making it possible to reproduce infi-nite copies of it—thus devaluing the "aura" of the original—Chow envisions the "native" himself as the original, with his own aura. When natives stop acting like natives—that is to say, when they de-viate from the stereotypes that have been set up to signify their identities—their "aura" is lost: they are no longer "authentic." Thus, a rationale for the existence of racial cybertypes becomes clear: in a virtual environment like the Internet where *everything* is a copy, so to speak, and nothing has an aura since all cyberimages exist as pure pixellated information, the desire to search for an orig-inal is thwarted from the very beginning. Hence the need for images of cybertyped "real natives" to assuage that desire. Chow poses a series of questions in this section:

Why are we so fascinated with "history" and with the "native" in "modern" times? What do we gain from our labor on these "endangered authenticities" which are presumed to be from a different time and a different place? What can be said about the juxtaposition of "us" (our discourse) and "them"? What kind of *surplus value* is created by this juxtaposition? (42)

The surplus value created by this juxtaposition (between the Western user and the discourses of race and racism in cyberspace) lies precisely within the need for the native in modern times. As machine-induced speed enters our lives—the speed of transmission of images and texts, of proliferating information, of dizzying arrays of decision trees and menus—all of these symptoms of modernity create a sense of unease that is remedied by comforting and familiar images of a "history" and a "native" that seems frozen in "a different time and a different place."

This is the paradox: In order to think rigorously, humanely, and imaginatively about virtuality and the "posthuman," it is absolutely necessary to ground critique in the lived realities of the human, in all their particularity and specificity. The nuanced realities of virtuality—racial, gendered, othered—live in the body, and though science is producing and encouraging different readings and revisions of the body, it is premature to throw it away just yet, particularly since so much postcolonial, political, and feminist critique stems from it.

The vexed position of women's bodies and raced bodies in feminist and postcolonial theory has been a subject of intense debate for at least the past twenty years. While feminism and postcolonial studies must, to some extent, buy into the notion of there being such a thing as a "woman" or a "person of color" in order to be coherent, there are also ways in which "essentialism is a trap," (89) to quote Gayatri Spivak. Since definitions of what counts as a woman or a person of color can be shifting and contingent upon hegemonic forces, essentialism can prove to be untenable. Indeed, modern body technologies are partly responsible for this: gender reassignment surgery and cosmetic surgery can make these definitions all the blurrier. In addition, attributing essential qualities to women and people of color can reproduce a kind of totalizing of identity that reproduces the old sexist and racist ideologies. However, Donna Haraway, who radically questions the critical gains to be gotten from conceptualizing *woman* as anchored to the body, takes great pains to emphasize that she does not "know of any time in history when there was greater need for political unity to confront effectively the dominations of 'race,' 'gender,' 'sexuality,' and 'class'" (157). Though she replaces the formerly essential concept of "woman" with that of the "cyborg," a hybrid of machine and human, she also acknowledges that feminist politics must continue "through coalition—affinity, not identity" (155). Both she and Spivak write extensively about the kinds of strategic affinities that can and must be built between and among "women" (albeit in quotation marks), racial and other minorities, and other marginalized and oppressed groups.

Is it a coincidence that just as feminist and subaltern politics—built around affinities as well as identities—are acquiring some legitimacy and power in the academy (note the increasing numbers of courses labeled "multicultural," "ethnic," "feminist," "postcolonial" in university course schedules) MCI Worldcom, and other teletechnology corporations are staking out their positions as forces that will free us from race and gender? Barbara Christian, in her 1989 essay "'The Race for Theory': Gender and Theory: Dialogues on Feminist Criticism," sees a similar kind of "coincidence" in regard to the increasing dominance of literary theory as a required and validated activity for American academics. She asserts that the technology of literary theory was made deliberately mystifying and dense to exclude minority participation; this exclusionary language "surfaced, interestingly enough, just when the literature of peoples of color, of black women, of Latin Americans, of Africans, began to move 'to the center'" (278). The user-unfriendly language of literary theory, with its poorly designed interfaces, overly elaborate systems, and other difficulties of access happened to arise during the historical moment in which the most vital and vibrant literary work was being produced by formerly "peripheral" minority writers.

Perhaps I am like Christian, who calls herself "slightly paranoid" in this essay (it has been well documented that telecommunications technologies encourage paranoia), but I too wonder whether cyberspace's claims to free us from our limiting bodies are not too well timed. Learning curves for Net literacy are notoriously high; those of us who maintain listservs and websites and multi-user domains (MUDs) learn that to our rue. Indeed, it took me a few years of consistent effort, some expensive equipment, and much expert assistance to feel anything less than utterly clueless in cyberspace. Rhetorics that claim to remedy and erase gender and racial injustices and imbalances through expensive and difficult-to-learn technologies such as the Internet entirely gloss over this question of access, which seems to me *the* important question. And it seems unlikely that this glossing over is entirely innocent. Cybertyping and other epiphenomena of high technologies in the age of the Internet are partly the result of people of color's restricted access to the means of production—in this case, the means of production of the "fluid identities" celebrated by so much theory and commerce today.

Increasing numbers of racial minorities and women are acquiring access to the Internet—a hopeful sign indeed. Ideally, this equalizing of access to the dominant form of information technology in our time might result in a more diverse cyberspace, one that doesn't seek to elide or ignore difference as an outmoded souvenir of the body. Indeed, sites such as ivillage.com, Oxygen.com, Salon.com's Hip Mama webpages, and NetNoir, which contain content specifically geared to women and to African Americans, indicate a shift in the Internet's content that reflects a partial bridging of the digital divide. As women of color acquire an increasing presence online, their particular interests, which spring directly from gender and racial identifications (that is to say, those identities associated with a physical body offline), are being addressed.

Unfortunately, as can be seen from the high, and ultimately dashed, feminist hopes that new media such as the Oxygen Network would express women's concerns in a politically progressive and meaningful way, gender and race can just as easily be co-opted by the e-marketplace. Commercial sites such as these tend to view women and minorities primarily as potential markets for advertisers and merchants rather than as "coalitions." Opportunities for political coalition building between women and people of color are often subverted in favor of e-marketing and commerce. (NetNoir is a notable exception to this trend. It is also the oldest of these identitarian websites, and thus was able to form its mission, content, and "look and feel" prior to the gold rush of dot-com commerce that brought an influx of investment capital, and consequent pressure to conform to corporate interests, to the web).[2] Nonetheless, this shift in content which specifically addresses women and minorities, either as markets or as political entities,[3] does acknowledge that body-related identities such as race and gender are not yet as fluid and thus disposable as much cybertheory and commercial discourse would like to see them.

However, such is the stubborn power of cybertyping that even when substantial numbers of racial minorities do have the necessary computer hardware and Internet access to deploy themselves "fluidly" online they are often rudely yanked back to the realities of racial discrimination and prejudice. For example, on March 13, 2000, in what was called "the first civil rights class action litigation against an Internet company," the Washington-based Equal Rights Center and two African-American plaintiffs sued Kozmo.com for racial "redlining" because of what was perceived as geographic discrimination (Katz n.p.). Kozmo.com, an online service that delivers convenience foods and products, claims to deliver only to "zip codes that have the highest rates of Internet penetration and usage" (Hamilton n.p.); however, the company's judgment of what constitutes an Internet-penetrated zip code follows racial lines as well. African-American Washingtonians James Warren and Winona Lake used their Internet access to order goods from Kozmo, only to be told that their zip codes weren't served by the company. Kozmo.com also refused to deliver to a neighborhood of Washington, D.C., occupied primarily by upper-class African Americans with equal "Internet penetration" as white neighborhoods (Prakash n.p.).[4] It seems that these African-American Internet users possessed identities online that were too firmly moored to their raced bodies to participate in the utopian ideal of the Internet as a democratizing disembodied space. Unfortunately, it would appear that online identities can never be truly fluid if one lives in the "wrong" zip code.

As the Kozmo.com example shows, actual hardware access is a necessary but not sufficient component of online citizenship. All of the things that citizenship implies—freedom to participate in community on an equal basis, access to national and local infrastructures, the ability to engage in discourse and commerce (cyber- and otherwise) with other citizens—are abrogated by racist politics disguised as corporate market research. This example of online redlining, or "refusing to sell something to someone due to age, race or location" puts a new spin on cybertyping. Rather than being left behind, bracketed, or "radically questioned" the body—the raced, gendered, classed body—gets "outed" in cyberspace just as soon as commerce and discourse come into play. Fluid identities aren't much use to those whose problems exist strictly (or even mostly) in the real world if they lose all their currency in the realm of the real.

It is common to see terms such as "body," "woman," and "race" in quotation marks in much academic writing today. The (after)images of identity that the Internet shows us similarly attempt to bracket off the gendered and raced body in the name of creating a democratic utopia in cyberspace. However, postmortems pronounced over "the body" are premature, as the Kozmo.com lawsuit shows. My hope is that these discourses of cyber-enabled fluidity and liberation do not grow so insular and self-absorbed as to forget this.

In the mechanical age, technology was viewed as instrumental, as a means to an end; users were figured as already-formed subjects who approach it, rather than contingent subjects who are approached and altered by it. However, this view has been radically challenged in recent years, in particular by the Internet and other telecommunications technologies, which claim to eradicate the notion of physical distance and firm boundaries not only between users and their bodies but between topoi of identity as well.

The Internet generates both images of identity and afterimages. The word *afterimage* implies two things to me in the context of contemporary technoscience and cyberculture.

The first is its a rhetorical position as a "Y2Kism," part of the millennial drive to categorize social and cultural phenomena as *post-*, as *after*. It puts pressure on the formerly solid and anchoring notion of identity as something we in the digital age are fast on our way to becoming "after." This notion of the posthuman has evolved in other critical discourses of technology and the body, and is often presented in a celebratory way.[5]

The second is this: the image that you see when you close your eyes after gazing at a bright light: the phantasmatic spectacle or private image gallery that bears but a tenuous relationship to "reality." Cyberspace and the images of identity that it produces can be seen as an interior, mind's-eye projection of the "real." I'm thinking especially of screen fatigue—the crawling characters or flickering squiggles you see inside your eyelids after a lot of screen-time in front of a television, cathode ray tube (CRT) terminal, movie screen, or any of the sources of virtual light to which we are exposed every day. How have the blinding changes and dazzlingly rapid developments of technology in recent years served to project an altered image or projection of identity upon our collective consciousness? This visual metaphor of the afterimage describes a particular kind of historically and culturally grounded seeing or misseeing, and this is important. Ideally, it has a critical valence and can represent a way of seeing differently, of claiming the right to possess agency in our ways of seeing—of being a subject rather than an object of technology. In the bright light of contemporary technology, identity is revealed to be phantasmatic, a projection of culture and ideology. It is the product of a reflection or a deflection of prior images, as opposed to afterimages, of identity. When we look at these rhetorics and images of cyberspace we are seeing an afterimage—both posthuman and projectionary—that is the product of a vision rearranged and deranged by the virtual light of virtual things and people.

Similarly, the sign-systems associated with advertisements for reproductive and "gendered" technologies reveal, in Valerie Hartouni's words, "the fierce and frantic iteration of conventional meanings and identities in the context of technologies and techniques that render them virtually unintelligible" (51). According to this logic, stable images of identity have been replaced by afterimages. When we look at cyberspace, we see a phantasm that says more about our fantasies and structures of desire than it does about the "reality" to which it is compared by the term *virtual reality*. Many of cyberspace's commercial discourses, such as the television and print advertisements I examine in closer detail in chapter 4, work on a semiotic level that establishes a sense of a national self. However, in a radically disruptive move they simultaneously deconstruct the notion of a corporeal self anchored in familiar categories of identity. Indeed, this example of "screen fatigue" (commercials are great examples of screen fatigue because they're so fatiguing) projects a very particular kind of afterimage of identity.

The discourse of many commercials for the Internet includes gender as only one of a series of outmoded "body categories" like race and age. The ungendered, deracinated self promised to us by these commercials is freed of these troublesome categories, which have been done away with in the name of a "progressive" politics. The goal of "honoring diversity" seen on so many bumper stickers will be accomplished by eliminating diversity.

It's not just commercials that are making these postidentitarian claims. Indeed, one could say that they're following the lead or at least running in tandem with some of the growing numbers of academics who devote themselves to the cultural study of technology. For example, in *Life on the Screen* Sherry Turkle writes,

> When identity was defined as unitary and solid it was relatively easy to recognize and censure deviation from a norm. A more fluid sense of self allows for a greater capacity for acknowledging diversity. It makes it easier to accept the array of our (and others') inconsistent personae—perhaps with humor, perhaps with irony. We do not feel compelled to rank or judge the elements of our multiplicity. We do not feel compelled to exclude what does not fit. (261)

According to this way of thinking, regulatory and oppressive social norms such as racism and sexism are linked to users' "unitary and solid" identities offscreen. Supposedly, leaving the body behind in the service of gaining more "fluid identities" means acquiring the ability to carve out new, less oppressive norms, and gaining the capacity to "acknowledge diversity" in ever more effective ways. However, is this really happening in cyberspace?

I answer this question with an emphatic no in chapter 2. I have coined the term *identity tourism* to describe a disturbing thing that I was noticing in an Internet chat community. During my fieldwork I discovered that the afterimages of identity that users were creating by adopting personae other than their own online as often as not participated in stereotyped notions of gender and race. Rather than "honoring diversity," their performances online used race and gender as amusing prostheses to be donned and shed without "real life" consequences. Like tourists who become convinced that their travels have shown them real "native" life, these identity tourists often took their virtual experiences as other-gendered and other-raced avatars as a kind of lived truth. Not only does this practice provide titillation and a bit of spice: as bell hooks writes, "one desires a 'bit of the Other' to enhance the blank landscape of whiteness" (29), it also provides a new theater in cyberspace for "eating the Other." For hooks, "the overriding fear is that cultural, ethnic, and racial differences will be commodified and offered up as new dishes to enhance the white palate—that the Other will be eaten, consumed, and forgotten" (39). Certainly, the performances of identity tourists exemplify the consumption and commodification of racial difference; the fact that so many users are willing to pay monthly service fees to put their racially stereotyped avatars in chat rooms attests to this.

REMASTERING THE INTERNET

The racial stereotype, a distinctive and ongoing feature of media generally, can be envisioned in archaeological terms. If we conceive of multimedia, in particular what's been termed the "new media" engendered by the Internet, as possessing strata—layers of accretions and amplifications of imageries and taxonomies of identity—then it is possible (and indeed, for reasons I will show shortly, *strategic*) to examine the structure of these layerings. Old media provide the foundation for the new, and their means of putting race to work in the service of particular ideologies is reinvoked, with a twist, in the new landscape of race in the digital age. Visions of a "postracial democracy" evident in much discourse surrounding the Internet (particularly in print and television advertisements), are symptomatic of the desire for a cosmetic cosmopolitanism that works to conceal the problem of racism in the American context.

I could put this another way: Where's the multi(culturalism) in multimedia? or Where is race in new media? What is the "work" that race does in cyberspace, our most currently privileged example of the technology of digital reproduction? What boundaries does it police? What "modes of digital identification" or disidentification are enabled, permitted, foreclosed vis-à-vis race? Has the notion of the "authentic" been destroyed permanently, a process that Benjamin predicted had begun at the turn of the century with the advent of new means of mechanical reproduction of images? How do we begin to understand the place of authenticity, in particular racial and cultural authenticity, in the landscape of new media? Digital reproduction produces new iterations of race and racialism, iterations with roots in those produced by mechanical reproduction. Images of race from older media are the analog signal that the Internet optimizes for digital reproduction and transmission.

On the one hand, Internet use can be seen as part of the complex of multimedia globalization, a foisting of a Western (as yet) cultural practice upon "third world," minority, and marginalized populations. Recent protests in the Western world against the International Monetary Fund critique global capitalism and globalization as not only economically exploitative of the "third world," but also culturally exploitative as well, essentially creating a "monoculture of the mind."

A recent full-page advertisement in the *New York Times* (June 19, 2000) uses the term *megatechnology* and superimposes it with an image of a television being carried on an African woman's head. (see fig. 1.1.) The ad copy reads, "Ours is the first culture in history to have moved inside media—to have largely replaced direct contact with people and nature for simulated versions on TV, sponsored by corporations. Now it's happening globally, with grave effects on cultural diversity and democracy." This advertisement, produced for the Turning Point Project, a coalition of more than eighty nonprofit organizations including Adbusters, the Media Alliance, the International Center for Technology Assessment, and the International Forum on Globalization, includes AOL Time Warner among the "biggest three global media giants" and explains that cultural diversity cannot survive virtual reality, of which television is cited as the "earliest form."

It claims that global media, including (especially) the Internet, produce a kind of "mental retraining; the cloning of all cultures to be alike." The positioning of this advertisement in a mainstream mass-media publication could seem to a cynical reader an exercise in bad faith, since the *New York Times* is itself a part of the global media complex the ad is critiquing. Nonetheless, the situatedness of

FIGURE 1.1. Monocultures of the Mind (Turning Point Project)

this argument within a nonacademic publication demonstrates that concerns about "virtual reality" or cyberspace as a culturally imperialistic practice exist outside of the academy as well as inside. Monocultures are posed here as the opposite of diversity. Ziauddin Sardar characterizes cyberspace itself as a monoculture, the West's "dark side" and thus a powerful continuation of the imperialist project. The discourse of agribusiness and the bioengineering of crops is central here: monocultures are economies of scale, an erasure of diversity under current attack by the fashionable as offering little resistance to disease. But where does the hybrid, specifically the "hyphenated" American of color, stand in relation to this?

In this ad, the image of the African woman in native dress walking a dusty road with a television balanced skillfully on her head is meant to be jarring, to operate as part of the argument against globalization, and against television watching in native cultures. Viewers are supposed to react with horror at the evil box contaminating her culture and the landscape. Yet, ought we (or do we) experience a similar horror when seeing a Filipino youth in Monterey Park, Los Angeles, carrying a boom box, break dancing, or eating a McDonald's hamburger? Or when we see a Chinese rock group performing in Britney Spears–type outfits? In the first example, vegetarians may well take offense, but the fact is that such sights are common, and are examples of what could be seen as resistant practices.

In the example with the African woman, the tourist gaze would like to see her outside of time, protected from the incursions of digital "culture" (or monoculture) by Western intervention: the authenticity of the timeless primitive is threatened by the television set. In the second example, cultural appropriations and borrowings are commonly celebrated as hybridity and assimilation. In the culture of popular music, the productive samplings, mixings, and remasterings of hip-hop are envisioned as vital signs of a flourishing youth culture. The technologies of contemporary music create a space for these cultural mixings, scratchings, and bricolage.

How do these paradigms from music fit the Internet? Does the Internet indeed create a monoculture? Is there space within it for the subaltern to speak? How do representations of the subaltern in reference to the Internet preserve or deny diversity? How is the paradigm of tourism invoked to stabilize threatened ideas of the authentic native post-Internet?

The Internet has a global sweep, a hype (hysteria?) attached to it; it makes distinctive claims to a radical postracial democracy that other media have failed to employ effectively. Racial cybertyping is at work on the Internet today, and its implications both *for* its "objects" and for the cultural matrix it is embedded in generally are far reaching. Groups such as racial and ethnic minorities, who are prone to being stereotyped in older media, are now being "remastered" to use more digital terminology, ported to cybertyping. Remastering, the practice of converting an analog signal—for instance, from a vinyl record, to a digital one like a digital video disc (DVD), or compact disk (CD), or to hypertext markup language (HTML)—preserves the "content" of the original piece while optimizing it for a new format. Remastering fiddles with sound levels and timbre, erases scratchy silences, smoothes roughnesses, and alters signal-to-noise ratios in such a way that the same song is made infinitely available for reproduction, replay, and retransmission. But with a difference: variations in tone, timbre, and nuance are detectable; while the song remains the same, some of its qualities are altered, as are the possibilities for different audiences, different occasions for capture, replay, and transmission. The weblike media complex of images of the racialized other as primitive, exotic, irremediably different, and fixed in time is an old song, one that the Internet has remastered or retrofit in digitally reproducible ways. I wish to get back in the studio, so to speak, and to see how this remastering happens and what its effects are upon social formations and readings of race in the age of digital reproduction. When you feed racism into this machine, what you get are images of "exotic" non-American racial minorities (but not American minorities) using technology.

The Internet is the fastest, most effective image-reproduction machine this world has yet seen. Just as the stereotype machine, that clumsy mechanical device that produced multiple but imperfect copies of an original image, has been replaced by more efficient and clearer, cleaner modes of image reproduction, so too are racial stereotypes being replaced by cybertypes. While racial stereotypes can now be perceived by our ever more discerning eyes as crude and obvious, and have thus have been appropriated as camp (as in

Bill Cosby's collection of racist black memorabilia), or parody (black humor, like Chris Rock's, turns upon this) or incorporated into a history of oppression, cybertypes have as yet managed to sneak under the radar of critical and popular scrutiny.[6] The digital images of natives, others, and the "raced" that proliferate on and around the Internet are clean, nonmechanical, and carried upon a beam of fiber-optic light. Cybertyping's phantom track can be traced in a Cisco television advertisement, produced as part of a series entitled "The Internet Generation" that participates in a subtle blend of racism and racialism. Rather than stereotyping different races, it cybertypes them. The children in the first ad, "Out of the Mouths of Babes," repeat statistics about the Internet's improvements about older media (i.e., "The Web has [*sic*] more users in the first five years than television did in the first thirty") in distinctively accented voices while they are depicted in "native" dress in "native" settings, such as a temple pool, a mosque, and a rural schoolyard. In addition, their dialogue is fractured, as each sentence is continued or repeated by a different child in a different locale. Thus, the ad tries to literalize the smaller world that Benjamin predicted audiences accustomed to proliferating mechanical images, and, by extension, digital images, would come to desire and expect. One child tells us that "a population the size of the United Kingdom joins the Internet every six months. Internet traffic doubles every one hundred days." This depiction of the Internet as a population one joins, rather than a service one purchases and consumes or a practice one engages in, significantly uses the ur-imperial nation, the United Kingdom, as the yardstick of measurement here. This language of a "united kingdom" of multiracial "generations" seems utopian, yet polices the racial and ethnic boundaries of this world very clearly. Global capitalism is envisioned as a United Nations of users from different countries united in their praise of the Internet, yet still preserved in their different ethnic dress, languages, and "look and feel."[7] Despite the fact that international Internet users are likely to be city dwellers, these ads depict them in picturesque and idealized "native" practices uncommon even in rural areas.

Cybertyping's purpose is to representatively bracket off racial difference, to assuage fears that the Internet is indeed producing a monoculture. The greater fear, however, which cybertyping actively works to conceal, is the West's reluctance to acknowledge its colonization of global media, and ongoing racist practices within its own borders. The ad's claims that "soon, all of our ideas will be free of borders" tries to stake out the notion that America's responsibility for its own problems with race, the greatest problem of our age in W. E. B. Du Bois's terms, will be erased when "borders" (between nations, between the mind and the raced body) are figuratively erased. The subtlety of this argument is necessary in our postcolonial, postmodern age: scenarios that invoke the scramble for Africa, an emblematic episode of the West's division and exploitation of the non-Western world, just will not "play" anymore. However, porting the imperialist impulse to a commercial like Cisco's "Generations" series, which cybertypes race as useful rather than divisive sneaks it under the surveillance cameras.

This commercial remasters race. Remastering implies subjugation, the recolonization of otherness in a "postcolonial" world, and its method rests upon the ideological rock of cultural "authenticity." On the contrary, rather than destroying authenticity, cybertyping wants to preserve it. Just as intellectuals in ethnic studies and women's studies are starting to radically question the efficacy of "authenticity" as a flag to rally around, a way to gain solidarity, the commercial discourse of the Internet (that is, the way it figures itself *to* itself) scrambles to pick up that dropped flag.

The Internet must contain images of authentic natives in the service of militating against particular images of cultural hybridity. The Internet functions as a tourism machine; it reproduces digital images of race as other. Missing from this picture is any depiction of race in the American context. The vexed question of racism here and now is elided. Racism is recuperated in this ad as cosmetic multiculturalism, or cosmetic cosmoplitanism. In this ad and others like it, American minorities are discursively fixed, or cybertyped, in particular ways to stabilize a sense of a cosmopolitan, digerati-privileged self, which is white and Western.

POSTRACIAL COSMOPOLITANISM

In "The Unbearable Whiteness of Being: African American Critical Theory and Cyberculture," Kalí Tal writes that "in cyberspace, it is

possible to completely and utterly disappear people of color," and
that the elision of questions of race in cyberspace has led to its
"whitinizing" (n.p.). On the contrary, race is far from elided in
these narratives; instead it is repurposed and remastered, made to
do new work. The following passage by James Fallows, taken from
"The New Poor," an article written for the *New York Times Magazine*, elucidates this:

> The tech establishment has solved, in a fashion, a problem
> that vexes the rest of America—and therefore thinks about it
> in a way that seems to prefigure a larger shift. The hallway
> traffic in any major technology firm is more racially varied
> than in other institutions in the country. (It is also over-
> whelmingly male.) But the very numerous black and brown
> faces belong overwhelmingly to immigrants, notably from
> India, rather than to members of American minority groups.
> The percentage of African-Americans and Latinos in profes-
> sional positions in booming tech businesses is extremely low,
> nearing zero at many firms. (95)
> [. . .]
> People in the tech world inhabit what they know to be a
> basically post-racial meritocracy. I would sit at a lunch table
> in the software firm with an ethnic Chinese from Malaysia on
> one side of me, a man from Colombia across the table and a
> man born in India but reared in America next to him. This
> seems, to those inside it, the way the rest of the world should
> work, and makes the entrenched racial problems of black-
> and-white American seem like some Balkan rivalry one is
> grateful to know is on the other side of the world. (95)

This article refers to the technological (and in this case Internet-
driven) diaspora of brown, black, and yellow foreign high-tech
workers into America's technology industry. This contributes to a
cosmetic multiculturalism, a false sense of racial equality—or postracial cybermeritocracy—that I would term *cosmetic multiculturalism*. As Fallows notes, this cosmetic multiculturalism actively works
to conceal "the entrenched racial problems of black and white
America." The presence of black and brown faces from other coun-

tries, notably Asian ones, encourages white workers to inhabit a *virtually* diverse world, one where local racial problems are shuffled aside by a *global* and disaporic diversity created by talented immigrants as opposed to "hyphenated Americans." This is a form of tourism, benefiting from difference in order to make the American/Western self feel well-rounded, cosmopolitan, *postracial*. This is not digital identification, but digital *dis*identification—disavowal of the recognition of race in local contexts in favor of comfortably distant global ones. In the new landscape of cyberspace, other countries (i.e., markets, and sources of cheap expert immigrant labor in information fields) exist, but not American minorities. It only seems commonsensical, as Reed Koch, a manager at Microsoft, puts it, that "if you go ten years [in the high-tech corporate world] and extremely rarely in your daily life ever encounter an American black person, I think they disappear from your awareness" (Fallows 95). One of the symptoms of cybertyping is this convenient "disappearance from awareness" of American racial minorities, a symptom that "multiculturalist" Internet advertising and the discourse of technology work hard to produce.

CYBERTYPING AND THE AMERICAN SCENE

In Vijay Prashad's important work *The Karma of Brown Folk*, he poses a question to Asian readers: "How does it feel to be the solution?" In this volume, Prashad invokes Du Bois's rhetorical question to African Americans—"How does it feel to be a problem?"—and repurposes it in order to trace the construction of the Asian, in particular the South Asian, as a model minority. The figure of the Asian as model worker is inextricably tied to this stereotype, which has been reiterated as a particular cybertype of the Asian as an exemplary information worker. If one sees race as a major "problem" of American digital culture, an examination of these cybertypes reveals the ways in which Asians prove to be the "solution." Different minorities have different functions in the cultural landscape of digital technologies. They are good for different kinds of ideological work. And, in fact, this taxonomy of work and identity has been remastered: seeing Asians as the solution and blacks as the problem is and has always been a drastic and damaging formulation which pits minorities against each other and is evident in the culture at large.

On the contrary, in a fascinating twist, cybertyping figures both Asians and blacks as the solution, but for different problems. While Asians are constructed as anonymous workers, an undifferentiated pool of skilled (and grateful) labor, African Americans serve as a semiotic marker for the "real," the vanishing point of cyberspace in particular and technology in general.[8]

THE NEW NEW THING:
HEAD-HUNTING THE SOUTH ASIAN CYBORG

The issue of the *New York Times Magazine* that contains Michael Lewis's article "The Search Engine" features a cover graphic that repeats the words "The New New Thing" hundreds of times. The subtitle is "How Jim Clark taught America what the techno-economy was all about." Clark, the founder of Netscape, Silicon Graphics, and Healtheon is described as "not so much an Internet entrepreneur as the embodiment of a new kind of economic man." This article reveals that the "new kind of economic man," specifically an American man, attains preeminence partly by his ability to repurpose the discourse of racism, to create new cybertypes of Asian technology workers, in ways which at first seem unobjectionable because they have become so common.

Clark spent a great deal of energy recruiting Indian engineers from Silicon Graphics (like engineer Pavan Nigam) to work for his new start-up Healtheon. As Lewis writes, "Jim Clark [of Netscape] had a thing for Indians. 'The Indian outcasts of Silicon Valley,' he usually called them, 'my Indian hordes' in less sober moments. 'As a concentrated group,' he said, 'they were the most talented engineers in the valley . . . *And they work their butts off*'" (Lewis 82).

These "less sober moments" reveal cybertyping in action. This idea of Indians as constituting a horde devoid of individuality, a faceless mob, reveals both a fear of their numbers and a desire to become the head of the horde, their leader.[9] These "Indian outcasts" are seen as a natural resource to be exploited—valuable workers, like Chinese railroad laborers. What's more, they're a racial group characterized "naturally" as always-already digital,

like Asians as a whole. In 1997, Bill Gates indulged in a moment of
foot-in-mouth cybertyping when he declared during a visit to India
that "South Indians are the second-smartest people on the planet
(for those who are guessing, he rated the Chinese as the smartest;
those who continue to guess should note that white people, like
Gates, do not get classified, since it is the white gaze, in this incarnation, that is transcendental and able to do the classifying!)"
(Prashad 70). Asian technology workers are thought not to need a
"personal life," just like Chinese railroad workers were thought to
have nerves farther away from the skin. This characterization of
Asians as being superior workers because of inherent, near-physio-
logical differences, seeing them as impervious to pain, in their butts
or elsewhere, places them squarely in a new, digital "different
caste": the outcasts of Silicon Valley. This term repurposes the old
language of caste, an ancient system that preserves hierarchical dis-
tributions of privilege and oppression, for use in the digital age.
Keeping to this logic, no amount of work can make them a part of
the digital economy as "entrepreneurs" or "new economic men";
they are figured as permanent outcasts and outsiders.[10] Yet, such is
the power of cybertyping that Clark's and Gates's comments are not
viewed as racist but as strategic, a canny recognition of the rightful
work of race in the digital age: this is what makes Clark the "new
economic man."

As Lisa Lowe writes, "stereotypes that construct Asians as the
threatening 'yellow peril,' or alternatively, that pose Asians as the
domesticated 'model minority,' are each equally indicative of these
national anxieties" (18). Clark's figuration of South Indian engineers, his "thing," cybertypes them as simultaneously, rather than
alternatively, the threatening horde *and* the model minority: both
threatening as a quasi-conspiratorial "concentrated group" and enticing because of their engineering talents. This cybertype of the
South Asian seeks to fix the "unfixed liminality of the Asian immigrant—geographically, linguistically, and racially at odds with the
context of the 'national'—that has given rise to the necessity of end-
lessly fixing and repeating such stereotypes" (Lowe 19).

Indeed, the discourse of Internet technology has a "thing" for
Asians. In the article noted above, Jim Clark describes himself as a
headhunter, and the term is appropriate in at least two senses of the

word. A headhunter, in the language of the cultural digerati, is an entrepreneur who locates professional "talent" and lures it away from one job to another. Much of the tension in this story has to do with Clark's quest to acquire Asian engineers he'd previously worked with for his new venture. A high-tech headhunter facilitates the flow of human capital and labor, often across national borders.[11] The term has roots in colonial discourse: a headhunter is a mythologized figure, like the cannibal, constructed by colonists to embody their notions of the native as savage, a creature so uncivilized and unredeemable that he cannot be broken of his habit of collecting humans as if they were trophies; thus he must be exterminated or civilized. The figure of the headhunter was a justification for colonization. Envisioning South Asians as if they were trophies, outcasts, or hordes, having a "thing for Indians," is a form of cybertyping; it homogenizes South Asians as a group in such a way that they constitute both the familiar model-minority paradigm as well as a resource for global capital. And what's more, cybertyping permits this kind of speech, even allows it to signify as "cool," or "new" in a way that Jimmy "the Greek" Synodinos's better-intentioned comments about the superiority of black athletes could not be.

As Lewis writes, "By 1996 nearly half of the 55,000 temporary visas issued by the United States government to high-tech workers went to Indians. The definitive smell inside a Silicon Valley start-up was of curry" (82). This insistence upon the smell of curry in the context of global commerce and capitalism works to discursively fix Asians as irredeemably foreign in order to stabilize a sense of a national self. This smell, here invoked as a stereotyped sign of South Asian identity, is figured as a benefit of sorts to white workers, a kind of virtual tourism: they need never leave their start-up offices (a frowned-upon practice in any event) yet can conveniently enjoy the exotic cuisine and odors of "another" world and culture.

At the dawn of the twenty-first century, cultural digerati live lives composed of these "less sober moments"; culturally and economically, Americans are living in intoxicating times, a gold rush of sorts. The fever of acquisition, creation, and entrepreneurship engendered by dot-com culture licenses specific forms of racialism, if not overt racism, that are no more descriptive of the lived realities of Asian immigrants or Asian Americans than earlier colonialist or racist ways of speaking were. Just as the gold rush depended upon the exploited labor of Chinese immigrants, black slaves, and Mexican workers and consequently created racial stereotypes to justify and explain their exploitation as "Western expansion," so too does our current digital gold rush create mythologies of race that are nostalgic. That is, they hark back to earlier narratives of race and racialism which were always-already "virtual" in the sense that they too were constructed narratives, the product of representational labor and work. As Susan Stewart defines nostalgia, it is a "sadness without an object." Nostalgia is "always ideological: the past it seeks has never existed except as narrative, and hence, always absent, that past continually threatens to reproduce itself as a felt lack" (23). The construction of postracial utopias enabled by the Internet, and so prominently troped in television advertising for the Internet, seeks to fill that "lack" by supplying us with new narratives of race that affirm its solidity in the face of global culture, multiracialism, and new patterns of migration. Cybertyping keeps race "real" using the discourse of the virtual. The object of digital nostalgia is precisely the idea of race itself. As Renato Rosaldo defines it, nostalgia is "often found under imperialism, where people mourn the passing of what they themselves have transformed," and is "a process of yearning for what one has destroyed that is a form of mystification" (quoted in hooks 25). Cybertyping works to rescue the vision of the authentic raced "native" that, first, never existed except as part of an imperialist set of narratives, and second, is already gone, or "destroyed" by technologies such as the Internet.

AFRICAN-AMERICAN DIGITAL DIVIDES: BAMBOOZLED BY THE MYTH OF ACCESS

The year 2000 was a banner year, for "Web use became balanced between sexes for the first time year with 31.1 million men and 30.2 million women online in April, according to Media Metrix. In some months this year [. . .] female users have significantly outnumbered their male counterparts" (Austen D7). The digital divide between the genders is shrinking, which is not to say that there isn't gender cybertyping occurring online. (This contradicts prior predictions from the early and mid-1990s that a masculinist web would repel women from logging on: on the contrary, as in television, sexism didn't repel women from the medium). The hegemony of the web is still emphatically male. However, the article from which these statistics come, entitled "Studies Reveal a Rush of Older Women to the Web," also notes that "lost in the rush to use the Web, however, are the nation's poor."

While the article provides graphs and statistics to track web use by gender, nationality, income, and whether users log on from home or work, it neglects to mention race as a factor at any point. This elision of race in favor of gender and class is symptomatic of what Radhika Gajjala sees as the tendency of "this upwardly mobile digiterati class to celebrate a romanticized 'multiculturalism' and diversity in cyberspace" (6).

It is widely assumed that the digital divide is created by inequities in access; indeed, institutional efforts to address this divide seem solely focused on getting everyone online as quickly as possible. African Americans are cybertyped as information "have-nots," occupying the "wrong" side of the digital divide; it tropes them as the "problem." This fallacy—that access equals fair representation in terms of race and gender—can be traced by examining the ways that race has worked in other media.

No sane person would contend that once everyone has cable, television will become a truly democratic and racially diverse medium, for we can see that this has not come to pass. Mainstream film and television depicts African Americans in consistently negative ways despite extremely high usage rates of television by African Americans. [12] Hence, the dubious goal of 100 percent "penetration" of African-American communities by Internet technologies cannot, by and of itself, result in more parity or even accuracy in representations of African Americans. How does the Internet perpetuate this myth of access-as-ultimate-equalizer? Cyberspace's rhetorics make claims that are distinctively different from those of other media: its claims to "erase borders" and magically produce equality simply via access can be seen nowhere else. However, Internet usage by racial minorities is a necessary, but not sufficient, condition of a meaningfully democratic Internet. As Spike Lee's brilliant film parody *Bamboozled* (2000) makes all too clear, even the presence of black writers or content producers in a popular medium such as television fails to guarantee programming that depicts "dignified black people" if audiences are unwilling to support the show in large numbers. In *Bamboozled*, the Harvard-educated black television writer Pierre Delacroix produces the most offensive, racist, "ignorant" variety show he can come up with as a form of revenge against his white boss. He fully intends that the show, which depicts blacks as Topsys, Aunt Jemimas, Sambos, and Little Nigger Jims, will be a resounding flop. He entitles it the *Man Tan New Millennium Minstrel Show* and requires the African American performers to appear in authentic blackface made of burnt cork. Of course, it is a major hit with the networks and the audience. This can be seen as an object lesson to people interested in the Internet's potential as a space for activism and antiracist education: what needs to happen on the Internet to ensure that it doesn't become the newest of the new millennium minstrel shows? The film contains a clip from Lee's earlier film, *Malcolm X*, in which the protagonist addresses a crowd of African Americans, crying out, "You been hoodwinked, bamboozled." Until we acquire some insight into racial cybertypes on the Internet, we are quite likely to be hookwinked and bamboozled by the images of race we see on the Net, images that bear no more relation to real people of color than minstrel shows do to dignified black people.

Due to the efforts of black activists and scholars working in older media studies, we can better see what's at stake in this limited range of representations of racial minorities. Studies of race and the Internet are just now beginning to catch up (which is not surprising, considering the familiar lag time in media criticism when it comes to critical readings of race).

We should wish Internet access for the betterment of material and educational conditions of African Americans, but ought not expect that the medium itself is going to represent them fairly without any strategies or plans put into place to encourage this direction.

POSTRACIAL DIGERATI? CYBERTYPING THE OTHER

Some studies claim that the Internet causes depression. A 1998 Carnegie Mellon University study posits that this is so because the Internet reduces the number of "strong social ties" that users maintain in "real life" and replaces them with "weak" or virtual ties, which don't have the same beneficial psychological effects as face-to-face social interactions (Kraut and Lundmark 1029). The Internet's ability to produce depression in its users (at least in me) can be traced at least in part to cybertyping, a kind of virtual social interaction that constructs people of color as "good" workers or "bad," on the "right" or "wrong" side of the digital divide. The Internet's claims to erase borders, such as gender, class, and racial divisions, and the ways in which public policy makers' attentions to bridging the "digital divide" that is erroneously attributed as being the source of these problems in representation, overshadow these more subtle varieties of cybertyping. This dynamic is indeed depressing, all the more so because largely silent and undiscussed.

Radhika Gajjala writes.

Race, gender, age, sexuality, geographical location and other signifiers of "Otherness" interact with this class-based construction of "whiteness" to produce complex hierarchies and contradictions within the Digital Economy. While we can continue to call this[4] "whiteness" because the status quo is still based upon a cultural hegemony that privileges a "white" race, it might be more appropriate to refer to this upwardly mobile subject as a "privileged hybrid transnational subject" who is a member of the "digiterati" class. (6)

Here, Gajjala posits that "privileged hybrid transnational subjects" such as Clark's coveted South Asian programmers can be read, for all intents and purposes, as "white" since they participate in the "cultural hegemony that privileges a white race." While they are no doubt part of that hegemony, as is every person of color who consumes, produces, and becomes the object of representation of information technologies, I contend that they are put to work in that hegemony in distinctively raced ways. The "work" that they do in this hegemony, their value-added labor in the system of information practices dubbed "global capitalism," is this: their cybertypes work to preserve taxonomies of racial difference. The nostalgia for race, or visions of racial "authenticity" invoked by the Cisco advertisements, assuages a longing. The espoused public desire for technological uplift, in the discourse of science-fiction narratives, the desire to create a new class of "digiterati" that is in some sense postracial, is matched by a corresponding longing for "race" as a spectacle of difference, a marker to function as the horizon to the vanishing point of postmodern identities.

Contemporary debates about the digital divide tend to be divided roughly into two camps. The first of these maintains that the master's tools can never dismantle the master's house, to paraphrase Audre Lorde's formulation. In other words, if people of color rush to assimilate themselves into computer culture, to bridge the digital divide, they are simply adopting the role of the docile consumer of Microsoft, Intel, and other products, and are not likely to transform the cyberspace they encounter. Like feminists who adopt the values of the patriarchy, they may succeed as isolated individuals in what has thus far been a privileged white male's domain—technology and the Internet—but cannot bring about the kind of change that would bring about true equality. As Lorde writes, taking up the master's tools "may allow us to temporarily beat him at his own game, but they will never allow us to bring about genuine change. And this fact is only threatening to those women who still define the master's house as their only source of support" (99).

The second camp maintains that people of color can only bring about "genuine change" in the often imperialistic images of race that exist online by getting online. Envisioning cybertechnologies as less the master's tools than tools for discourse that can take any shape is an optimistic ways of seeing things.

While it is impossible to say, definitively, which path is correct, there is no question that the digital divide is both a result of and a contributor to the practice of racial cybertyping. It is crucial that we continue to scrutinize the deployment of race online as well as the ways that Internet use can figure as a racialized practice if we are to realize the medium's potential as a vector for social change. There is no ignoring that the Internet can and does enable new and insidious forms of racism. Whether the master's tools present the best way to address this state of affairs has yet to be seen.

< 2 >

HEAD-HUNTING ON THE INTERNET: IDENTITY TOURISM, AVATARS, AND RACIAL PASSING IN TEXTUAL AND GRAPHIC CHAT SPACES

Is it accurate to say that on the Internet nobody can tell what race you are? For the large (and increasing) number of people who use the Internet as a social space via chat rooms and other forms of online interaction, this seemingly philosophical question has acquired increasing urgency. Despite claims by digital utopians that the Internet is an ideally democratic, discrimination-free space—without gender, race, age, or disability—an analysis of both textual and graphic chat spaces such as LambdaMOO, Time Warner's The Palace, and Avaterra's Club Connect will reveal that these identity positions are still very much in evidence. Though it is true that users' physical bodies are hidden from other users, race has a way of asserting its presence in the language users employ, in the kinds of identities they construct, and in the ways they depict themselves online, both through language and through graphic images. These depictions of the self, or online identities, have been termed "avatars." Avatars are the embodiment, in text and/or graphic images, of a user's online presence in social spaces.

The Internet is a theater of sorts, a theater of performed identities. "Passing" is a cultural phenomenon that has the ability to call stable identities into question, and in that sense can be a progressive practice. but the fact remains that passing is often driven by harsh structural cultural inequities, a sense that it really *would* be safer. more powerful, and better to be of a different race or gender.

Millions of computer users "pass" every day, and much scholarly work has been devoted to examining how, why, and what it means that this happens in relation to gender. Piles of articles have been written about cross-gender passing, or "computer cross-dressing," but very little has been done on the topic of cross-racial passing despite the fact it may be as common, or even more so. I read this notable *lack* of research on race in cyberspace springing in part from the "digital divide"—that is, the relative lack of computer and network access for racial minorities in comparison to whites.

The celebration of the Internet as a democratic, "raceless" place needs to be interrogated, both to put pressure on the assumption that race is something that *ought* to be left behind, in the best of all possible cyberworlds, and to examine the prevalence of racial representation in this supposedly unraced form of social and cultural interaction.

If race is indeed a cultural construct rather than a biological fact, as Anthony Appiah and others have asserted, then cyberspace is a particularly telling kind of example when we wish to look at the vexed and contested position of race in the digital age. The Internet is literally a "construct" (as the recent film *The Matrix* terms it); like race itself, it is a product of culture and its attendant power dynamics rather than an object that somehow existed prior to linguistic and cultural definition. Cyberspace is a place of wish fulfillments and myriad gratifications, material and otherwise, and nowhere is this more true than in chat spaces. Both textual and graphic chat spaces encourage users to build different identities, to take on new nicknames, and to describe themselves in any way they wish to appear. Digital avatars, or renditions of self, provide a pipeline into the phantasmatic world of identities, those conscious or not-so-conscious racial desires and narratives that users construct and inhabit during their interactions in cyberspace.

When I first started researching the topic of race and cyberspace in 1993, the World Wide Web was still a text-only phenomenon: no images were available. Thus, early chat room participants had recourse only to text when they constructed their avatars. Nicknames like Asian_Geisha, Big10inch, and GeekKing were accompanied by often floridly written self-descriptions that advertised not who users "really" *were*, but rather what they wanted (which in some sense may boil down to the same thing). These textual self-portraits had to do all of the work of physical description, since there were no images available. Race was invisible unless a player chose to inscribe it or include it in their her character description, and since many did not, a kind of default whiteness reigned. A great deal of scholarly work has been done on text-only MOOs and MUDs since then, much of it about LambdaMOO.[1]

However, the World Wide Web's dominance of the Internet has transformed cyberspace into a world of visual images, a world in which text has taken a backseat. Graphic avatars are *visible*, and thus race, which was invisible in textual avatars unless specifically put there, became visible as well. Websites that support graphic avatars like Time Warner's The Palace and Avaterra's Worlds Away Club Connect allow users to create images of themselves that they can move through cyberspace and customize. In this way, graphic chat resembles a video game more than it does live action e-mail in the sense that other users can see you and interact with you as an image. Online graphic role-playing in games such as Ultima Online and EverQuest have proven wildly popular with users; even though it costs $9.95 a month "to maintain a player, or 'avatar' in Britannia," one of Ultima Online's virtual worlds, "U.O. is one of the few unambiguously profitable uses of the Internet other than pornography" (Kolbert 92). Clearly, users are eager to pay additional fees (on top of Internet service provider subscription costs) to join the "quarter of a million people [who] subscribe" to Ultima Online, one of many commercial graphic chat spaces (Kolbert 90). Indeed, "electronic gaming has moved ahead at an improbable speed. Now, between the sales of consoles and those of software, it is a business larger than Hollywood" (Kolbert 88). Though MMPOGs, or "massively multi-player online games," constitute only a subset of the category known as "electronic gaming," their growing popularity attests to the appeal of visual avatars as theatrical prostheses in cyberspace.

Club Connect, a graphic chat space run by Avaterra, a company specializing in web-based business meeting spaces, can be accessed via its direct link from NetNoir's website. NetNoir is probably the oldest and certainly one of the best-known examples of an ethnic-identity website, which makes it a rare and important example of a minority presence on the web and the Internet in general. NetNoir started out as a text-only bulletin board addressing African-American concerns, and though it is less than five years old, it is still about as venerable as a website can be. (It is well known that Internet years are like "dog years": one of them might equal seven in "normal" time). I wanted to experience graphic chat through a minority-run website to see if this factor might prove an exception to the overwhelming whiteness I had seen on the Internet in general. I wish I could say that it did, but unfortunately it didn't, or rather only did in fairly limited ways. As Thomas Foster writes, "Virtual reality privileges vision as a mode of information processing, and visual perception remains inextricably linked to a history of racial stereotyping" (160). When contrasting graphic chat with earlier forms of text-only chat, such as LambdaMOO, it can be seen that the more image-rich "virtual reality" enabled by the superior bandwidth it employs only intensifies the "privileging of vision as a mode of information processing," and consequently produces racial and gendered cybertypes of the body that can come across as potentially and perhaps perniciously more "real" than their textual counterparts. A case in point: "Starr Long, cocreator of Ultima Online, remembered his own reaction when he learned prostitution had been introduced. 'Awesome!'" (Kolbert 98). This somewhat disturbing reaction makes perfect sense when we consider the game designers' priorities when creating these immensely popular online social environments: Long's jubilance is due to the fact that spontaneous development of such practices as prostitution online attests to the "realness" of the Internet environment. Prostitution means that the illusion of bodies created in Ultima Online *works* for the players; sex and gender, like race, need bodies—or rather, "visual perceptions" that readers can *take* as bodies—in order to possess virtual currency. Unfortunately, cybertyping flourishes under these same conditions; racism, prostitution, and other forms of identity-based oppression online become possible (and perhaps inevitable) when visual perceptions are informed by the same sets of objectifying ideologies that inform these activities offline.

LambdaMOO AND ORIENTALISM

A cute cartoon dog sits in front of a computer, gazing at the monitor and typing away busily. The cartoon's caption jubilantly proclaims, "On the Internet, nobody knows you're a dog!" This image resonates with particular intensity for those members of a rapidly expanding subculture that congregates within the consensual hallucination defined as cyberspace. Users define their presence within this textual and graphic space through a variety of different activities—commercial interaction, academic research, netsurfing, real-time interaction and chatting with interlocutors who are similarly "connected"—but all can see the humor in this image because it illustrates so graphically a common condition of being and self-definition within this space. Internet users represent themselves within it solely through the medium of keystrokes and mouse clicks, and through this medium they can describe themselves and their physical bodies any way they like; they perform their bodies as text.

On the Internet, nobody knows you're a dog; it is possible to "computer cross-dress" and represent yourself as a different gender, age, or race (Stone 84). In millennium America, this supposedly radically democratic aspect of the Net is celebrated frequently and unconditionally. The cartoon celebrates access to the Internet as a social leveler that permits even dogs to freely express themselves in discourse to their masters, who are deceived into thinking that dogs are their peers rather than their property. The element of difference, in this cartoon the difference between species, is comically subverted in this image; in the medium of cyberspace, distinctions and imbalances in power between beings who perform themselves solely through writing seem to have been deferred, if not effaced.

This utopian vision of cyberspace as a promoter of a radically democratic form of discourse should not be underestimated. Yet the image can be read on several levels. The freedom of which the dog chooses to avail itself is the freedom to "pass" as part of a privileged group—human computer users with access to the Internet. This is possible because of the discursive dynamic of the Internet, particularly in chat spaces like LambdaMOO, where users are known to others by self-authored names they give their "characters" rather than the more revealing e-mail addresses that include domain names. Defining gender is a central part of the discourse—players who choose to present themselves as "neuter," one of the several genders available to players on LambdaMOO, are often asked to "set gender," as if the choice to have a neuter gender is not a choice at all, or at least one that other players choose to recognize. They are seen as having deferred a choice rather than having made an unpopular one. This is an example of the "informatics of domination" that Donna Haraway describes in *Simians, Cyborgs, and Women*.[2] Gender is an element of identity that must be defined by each player, though the creators of LambdaMOO try to contribute toward a reimagining of gender by offering four choices (two more than are acknowledged in "real life"); still, one must be chosen. Each player must enunciate a chosen gender, since this gender will be visible to all players who call up other players' physical descriptions on their screens. Race, however, is not an option that must be chosen. Although players can elect to write it into their descriptions, it is not required by the programming that they do so.

Nonetheless, race is "written" in role-playing cyberspaces as well as read by other players. It is crucial to direct critical attention toward the conditions under which race is enunciated, contested, and ultimately erased and suppressed online, and the ideological implications of these performative acts of writing and reading otherness. What does the way race is written in cyberspace reveal about the enunciation of difference in new electronic media? Have the rules of the game changed, and if so, how?

Role-playing sites on the Internet offer their participants programming features such as the ability to physically "set" one's gender, race, and physical appearance, through which one can, and indeed in many cases is required to, project a version of the self that is inherently theatrical. Since true identities of interlocutors at Lambda are unverifiable (except by crackers and hackers, whose outlaw manipulations of code are unanimously construed by the Internet's citizens as a violation of both privacy and personal freedom) it can be said that everyone who participates is "passing," since it impossible to tell if a character's description matches a player's physical characteristics. Some of the uses to which this infixed theatricality are put are benign and even funny. Descriptions of self as a human-size pickle or pot-bellied pig are not uncommon, and generally are received in a positive, amused, tolerant way by other players. In contrast to this, players who elect to describe themselves in racially "othered" terms, as Asian, African American, or Latino, are often seen as engaging in a form of hostile performance, since they introduce what many consider a real-life "divisive issue" into the phantasmatic world of cybernetic textual interaction. The borders and frontiers of cyberspace, which had previously seemed so amorphous, take on a keen sharpness when the enunciation of racial otherness is put into play as performance. While everyone is "passing," some forms of racial passing are practiced and condoned because they do not threaten the integrity of a national sense of self that is defined as white.

The first act a participant in LambdaMOO performs is that of writing a self-description. It is the primal scene of cybernetic identity, a postmodern performance of the mirror stage:

> Identity is the first thing you create in a MUD. You have to decide the name of your alternate identity—what MUDders call your character. And you have to describe who this character is, for the benefit of the other people who inhabit the same MUD. By creating your identity, you help create a world. Your character's role and the roles of the others who play with you are part of the architecture of belief that upholds for everybody in the MUD the illusion of being a wizard in a castle or a navigator aboard a starship: the roles give people new stages on which to exercise new identities, and their new identities affirm the reality of the scenario. (Rheingold 148)

LambdaMOO requires that one choose a gender; though two of the choices are variations on the theme of "neuter," the choice cannot be deferred because the programming code requires it. It is impossible to receive authorization to create a character without making this choice. Race, on the other hand, is not only not a required choice, it is not even on the menu.[3] Players are given as many lines of text as they like to write any sort of textual description of themselves that they want. The architecture of belief that underpins social interaction in the MOO—that is, the belief that one's interlocutors possess distinctive human identities that coalesce through and vivify the glowing letters scrolling down the computer screen—is itself built upon this form of fantastic autobiographical writing. The majority of players in LambdaMOO do not mention race at all in their self-description, though most do include eye and hair color, build, age, and pronouns that indicate a male or a female gender. In those cases when race is not mentioned as such, but hair and eye color is, race is still being evoked—a character with blue eyes and blond hair will be assumed to be white. Yet while the textual conditions of self-definition and self-performance would seem to permit players total freedom, within the boundaries of the written word, to describe themselves in any way they choose, this choice is actually an illusion.

This is because the decision to leave race out of self-description does in fact constitute a choice: in the absence of racial description, all players are assumed to be white. This is partly due to the demographics of Internet users; most are white, male, highly educated, and middle class. It is also due to the utopian belief-system prevalent in the MOO. This system, which claims that the MOO should be a free space for play, strives toward policing and regulating racial discourse in the interest of social harmony. This system of regulation does permit racial role-playing when it fits within familiar discourses of racial stereotyping, and thus perpetuates these discourses. I am going to focus on Asian performance within the MOO because Asian personae are by far the most common nonwhite ones chosen by players and thus offer the greatest number of examples for study.

The vast majority of male Asian characters deployed in the MOO fit into familiar stereotypes from popular electronic media such as video games, television, and film, and popular literary genres such as science fiction and historical romance. Characters named Mr. Sulu, Chun Li, Hua Ling, Anjin San, Musashi, Bruce Lee, Little Dragon, Nunchaku, Hiroko, Miura Tetsuo, and Akira invoke their counterparts in the world of popular media. Mr. Sulu is the token Asian American in the television show *Star Trek*; Hua Ling and Hiroko are characters in the science-fiction novels *Eon* and *Red Mars*; Chun Li and Liu Kang are characters from the video games *Street Fighter* and *Mortal Kombat*; the movie star Bruce Lee was nicknamed "Little Dragon"; Miura Tetsuo and Anjin San are characters in James Clavell's popular novel and TV miniseries *Shogun*; Musashi is a medieval Japanese folklore hero; and Akira is the title of a Japanese anime film. The name Nunchaku refers to a weapon, as do, in a more oblique way, all of the names listed above. These names all adapt the samurai warrior fantasy for role-playing, and permit their users to perform a notion of the oriental warrior adopted from popular media. The effect of popular media in cyberspace has been to create a bricolage of figurations and simulations. The orientalized male persona, complete with sword, confirms the idea of the Asian man as potent, antique, exotic, and anachronistic.

This type of orientalized theatricality is a form of identity tourism; my research indicates that players who choose this type of racial play are almost always white, and their appropriation of stereotyped male Asian samurai figures allows them to indulge in a dream of crossing over racial boundaries temporarily and recreationally. Choosing these orientalized cybertypes tips their interlocutors off to the fact that they are not "really" Asian; they are instead playing in a familiar type of performance. Thus, the Orient is brought into the discourse, but only as a token or type. The idea of a nonstereotyped Asian male identity is so seldom enacted in LambdaMOO that its absence can only be read as a symptom of suppression.

The psychic motivations behind the desire to pass are explored by Kaja Silverman in her essay on *Blade Runner*, a film that interrogates some of the ways that technology blurs the borders between human and inhuman, artificial and authentic. The essay, "Back to the Future," locates the subject's desire to appropriate images of otherness through mimicry within a Lacanian framework that posits that "that transaction which is at the heart of all subjectivity, a transaction without which there could be no 'me'—[assumes] the image of the other" (127). The tokens and types of Asian maleness are pressed into service by identity tourists as a means to shore up their own subject positions online. Cyberspace is a disembodied place: the need to create very clear, recognizable personae is thus a practical one: coherent discourse demands that one is able to conceptualize a self that is *different* from its interlocutors. However, in constructing this necessary difference, the subject has recourse only to those markers of difference that already exist within the symbolic order. That is to say, users are drawn to create personae that are culturally coherent and intelligible, and racial cybertypes provide familiar, solid, and reassuring versions of race which other users can readily accept and understand since they are so used to seeing them in novels, films, and video games. This is not to say that online audiences particularly approve of the spectacle of virtual samurai and geishas in online environments; however, their presence does not constitute a threat to the idea of the subject as Western, white, and male. Indeed, the presence of images of the Orient works to enhance a user's sense of himself as the *one*, not the *other*. These images provide the necessary contrast, the dark background, against which the user can feel even more "himself" than he did before.

I wish to historicize the argument somewhat by emphasizing that in the contemporary cultural landscape, popular media such as video games, films, and television provide a rich but narrow repertoire of signifiers that mark Asian male difference. These tend to be anachronistic, mythic, and racist. Hence, the identity tourist cobbles together a rigidly "Asian" persona that possesses the cultural coherency common to all stereotypes in order to shore up his sense of self. His desire to create a "me" in cyberspace reflects the Lacanian subject's need to "assume the image of the other."

FANTASY TOURISM

Tourism is a particularly apt metaphor for describing the activity of racial identity appropriation in cyberspace. The term used to describe movement through cyberspatial sites—that is, "surfing" (an activity already associated with tourism in the minds of most Americans)—reinforces the idea that cyberspace is a place where travel and mobility are featured attractions, and figures it as a form of travel that is inherently recreational, exotic, and exciting. The choice to enact oneself as a samurai warrior in LambdaMOO constitutes identity tourism that allows a player to appropriate an Asian racial identity without any of the risks associated with being a racial minority in real life. While this might seem to offer a promising venue for non-Asian characters to see through the eyes of the other by performing themselves as Asian through online textual interaction, the fact that the personae chosen are overwhelmingly Asian stereotypes blocks this possibility by reinforcing these stereotypes.

This theatrical fantasy of identity tourism has deep roots in colonial narratives such as Rudyard Kipling's *Kim*, T. E. Lawrence's *Seven Pillars of Wisdom*, and Sir Richard Burton's writings. The Irish orphan and spy Kim, who uses disguise to pass as Hindu, Muslim, and other varieties of Indian natives, experiences the pleasures and dangers of cross-cultural performance. Edward Said's insightful reading of the nature of Kim's adventures contrasts the possibilities for play and pleasure for white travelers in an imperialistic world controlled by European empires with the relatively constrained plot resolutions offered that same boy back home: "For what one cannot do in one's own Western environment, where to try to live out the grand dream of a successful quest is only to keep coming up against one's own mediocrity and the world's corruption and degradation, one can do abroad. Isn't it possible in India to do everything, be anything, go anywhere with impunity?" (Said 42) To practitioners of identity tourism, LambdaMOO represents a phantasmatic and policed imperial space, much like Kipling's Anglo-India, which supplies a stage upon which the "grand dream of a successful quest" can be enacted.

Since the incorporation of the computer into the white-collar workplace, the line that divides work from play has become increasingly fluid. It is difficult for employers, and indeed for employees, to differentiate between doing research on the Internet and playing: exchanging e-mail, checking library catalogs, interacting with friends and colleagues through synchronous media like online conferencing and videoconferencing offer enhanced opportunities for gossip, jokes, and other distractions under the guise of work.[4] Time spent on the Internet is a hiatus from real life, or "RL," as it is called by most participants in virtual social spaces like LambdaMOO. When that time is spent in a role-playing space such as Lambda, devoted only to social interaction and the creation and maintenance of a convincingly "real" milieu modeled after an international community, that hiatus becomes a full-fledged vacation. That Lambda offers players the ability to write their own descriptions, as well as the fact that players often utilize this programming feature to write stereotyped Asian personae for themselves, reveals the attractions lying not only in being able to "go" to exotic spaces, but in co-opting the exotic and attaching it to oneself, to "becoming" it. The appropriation of racial identity becomes a form of recreation, a vacation from fixed identities and locales.

This vacation offers the satisfaction of a desire to fix the boundaries of cultural identity and exploit them for recreational purposes. As Said notes, the tourist who passes as the marginalized Other during his travels partakes of a fantasy of social control, one that depends upon and fixes the familiar contours of racial power relations:

> It is the wish-fantasy of someone who would like to think that everything is possible, that one can go anywhere and be anything. T. E. Lawrence in *The Seven Pillars of Wisdom* expresses this fantasy over and over, as he reminds us how he— a blond and blue-eyed Englishman—moved among the desert Arabs as if he were one of them. I call this a fantasy because, as both Kipling and Lawrence endlessly remind us, no one—least of all actual whites and non-whites in the colonies—ever forgets that "going native" or playing the Great Game are facts based on rock-like foundations, those of European power. Was there ever a native fooled by the blue or green-eyed Kims and Lawrences who passed among the inferior races as agent adventurers? I doubt it [. . .] (44)

Donna Haraway notes that high technologies "promise ultimate mobility and perfect exchange—and incidentally enable tourism, that perfect practice of mobility and exchange, to emerge as one of the world's largest single industries" (168). Identity tourism in cyberspaces like LambdaMOO functions as a fascinating example of the promise of high technology to enhance travel opportunities by redefining what constitutes travel. Logging onto a discursive space where one can appropriate exotic identities means that one need never cross a physical border or even leave one's armchair to go on vacation. In "'McDisneyization' and 'Post-Tourism': Contemporary Perspectives on Contemporary Tourism," George Ritzer and Allan Liska identify the Internet as a technologically enabled medium that will usher us into the age of "posttourism": "whatever happens, tourism will continue to flourish, but the McDonaldization thesis leads us to believe that, at least for some time, anticipatory technologies [. . .] such as videos, the Internet and especially virtual (or techno-) touring will not only prepare people to travel, but will replace journeys to far off locales" (101). This promise of post-touristic "ultimate mobility and perfect exchange" is not, however, fulfilled for everyone in LambdaMOO. The suppression of racial discourse that does not conform to familiar stereotypes, and the enactment of cybertyped notions of the oriental that do conform to them, extends the promise of mobility and exchange only to those who wish to change their identities to fit accepted norms.

Performances of Asian female personae in LambdaMOO are doubly repressive because they enact an identity tourism that cuts across the axes of gender and race, linking them in a powerful mix that brings together virtual sex, orientalist stereotyping, and performance. A listing of some of the names and descriptions chosen by players who masquerade as Asian females in LambdaMOO include Asian Doll, Miss Saigon, Bisexual Asian Guest, Michelle Chang, Geisha Guest, and Maiden Taiwan. They describe themselves as, for example, a "mystical Oriental beauty, drawn from the pages of a Nagel calendar," or in the case of Geisha Guest, a character owned by a white American man living in Japan:

> A petite Japanese girl in her twenties. She has devoted her entire life to perfecting the tea ceremony and mastering the art of lovemaking. She is multi-orgasmic. She is wearing a pastel kimono, 3 under-kimonos in pink and white. She is not wearing panties, and that would not be appropriate for a geisha. She has spent her entire life in the pursuit of erotic experiences.

It is commonly known that the relative dearth of women in cyberspace results in a great deal of "computer cross-dressing," or men masquerading as women. Men who do this are generally seeking sexual interaction, or "Netsex," from other players of both genders. When the performance is doubly layered, and users extend their identity tourism across both race and gender, it is possible to observe a double appropriation or objectification that uses the oriental as part of a sexual lure, thus using passing performances to exploit and reify the Asian woman as submissive, docile, and a sexual plaything. Beyond LambdaMOO, the fetishization of the Asian woman extends into other parts of the Internet. The extremely active Usenet news group called "alt.sex.fetish.orientals" is only one of the infamous alt.sex news groups that overtly focus upon race as an adjunct to sexuality.

PROSTHETIC BORDERS

Cyberspace is the newest incarnation of the idea of national boundaries. It is a phenomenon more abstract yet at the same time more "real" than outer space, since millions of participants immerse themselves in it daily while space travel has been experienced by only a few people. The term "cyberspace" participates in a topographical trope which, as Allucquère Rosanne Stone points out, defines the activity of online interaction as a taking place within a locus, a space, a world unto itself (104). This "second world," like a carnival, possesses constantly fluctuating boundaries, frontiers, and dividing lines that separate it from both the realm of the "real" (that which takes place offline) and its corollary, the world of the physical body which gets projected, manipulated, and performed via online interaction. The title of the *Time* magazine cover story for July 25, 1994—"The Strange New World of Internet: Battles on the Frontiers of Cyberspace"—is typical of the popular media's depictions of the Internet as a world unto itself with shifting frontiers and borders that are contested in the same way that national borders are. The "battle" over borders takes place on several levels that have been well documented elsewhere, such as the battle over encryption, and the conflict between the right of a private individual to transmit and receive information freely and the rights of government to monitor potentially dangerous, subversive, or obscene material that crosses state lines over telephone wires or fiber-optic cables. These contests concern the distinction between public and private. It is, however, seldom acknowledged that the trope of the battle on the cyberfrontier also connotes a conflict on the level of cultural self-definition. If, as Chris Chesher notes, "the frontier has been used since as a metaphor for freedom and progress, and . . . space exploration, especially, in the 1950s and 1960s was often called the "new frontier" (18), the figuration of cyberspace as the most recent representation of the frontier sets the stage for border skirmishes in the realm of cultural representations of the other. The discourse of space travel during this period solidified the American identity by limning out the contours of a cosmic—or "last"—frontier.[5] The "race for space," or the race to stake out a border to be defended against both the nonhuman (aliens) and the non-American (the Soviets), translates into an obsession with race and a fear of racial contamination, always one of the distinctive features of the imperialist project. In films such as *Alien*, the integrity and solidity of the American body is threatened on two fronts—both the antihuman (the alien) and the passing-as-human (the cyborg) seek to gain entry and colonize the character Ripley's human body. Narratives that locate the source of contaminating elements within a deceitful and uncanny technologically enabled theatricality—the ability to pass as human—depict performance as an occupational hazard of the colonization of any space. New and futuristic technologies call into question the integrity of categories of the human since they enable the nonhuman to assume a human face and identity.

In 1995 a character on Lambda named Tapu proposed a piece of legislation to the Lambda community in the form of a petition. This petition, entitled "Hate Crime," was intended to impose penalties upon characters who harassed other characters on the basis of race. The players' publicly posted responses to this petition, which failed by a narrow margin, reveals a great deal about the particular variety of utopianism characteristic of real-time textual online social interaction. The petition's detractors argued that legislation or discourse designed to prevent or penalize racist hate speech were unnecessary since those offended in this way had the option to hide their race by removing it from their descriptions. A character named Taffy wrote, "Well, who knows my race unless I tell them? If race isn't important than why mention it? If you want to get in somebody's face with your race then perhaps you deserve a bit of flak. Either way I don't see why we need extra rules to deal with this." Taffy, who signs himself "proud to be a sort of greyish pinky color with bloches [*sic*]," recommends a strategy of both blaming the victim and suppressing race, an issue that "isn't important" and should not be mentioned because doing so "get[s] in somebody's face." Fear of the flak supposedly generated by players' decisions to include race in their descriptions of self was echoed in another post to the same group by Nougat, who asked,

> [H]ow is someone to know what race you are a part of? [Is] this bill [. . .] meant to combat comments [. . .] towards people of different races, or just any comments whatsoever? Seems to me, if you include your race in your description, you are making yourself the sacrificial lamb. I don't include 'caucasian' in my description, simply because I think it is unnecessary. And thusly, I don't think I've ever been called "honkey."

Both of these posts emphasize that race is not, and should not be, necessary to social interaction on LambdaMOO. The punishment for introducing this extraneous and divisive issue into the MOO, which represents a vacation space, a fantasy island for its users, is to become a "sacrificial lamb." The attraction of a fantasy island lies in its ability to provide scenarios for the fantasies of privileged individuals. The maintenance of this fantasy, that of a race-free society, can only occur by suppressing forbidden identity choices.

DEFAULT WHITENESS

While many members of online social communities like LambdaMOO are stubbornly utopian in their attitudes toward the power dynamics and flows of information within the technologically mediated social spaces they inhabit, many of the academic theorists are pessimistic. Andrew Ross and Constance Penley introduce their collection *Technoculture* by asserting that "the odds are firmly stacked against the efforts of those committed to creating technological countercultures" (xiii). Chesher concedes, "In spite of the claims that everyone is the same in virtual worlds, access to technology and necessary skills will effectively replicate class divisions of the rest of reality in the virtual spaces" and "will tend to reinforce existing inequalities, and propagate already dominant ideologies" (28,

29). Indeed, the cost of Net access does contribute toward class as well as racial divisions. One of the dangers of identity tourism is that it takes this restriction across the axes of race/class in the "real world" to an even more subtle and complex degree by reducing nonwhite identity positions to part of a costume or masquerade to be used by curious vacationers in cyberspace. Asianness is co-opted as a passing fancy, an identity-prosthesis that signifies exotic sexual availability when female, and anachronistic dreams of combat when male. Self-identification as a samurai or geisha is diverting, reversible, and a privilege mainly used by white men. The paradigm of Asian transvestism on LambdaMOO itself works to suppress racial difference by setting the tone of the discourse in racist contours, which inevitably discourage "real life" Asian men and women from textual performance in that space, effectively driving race underground. As a result, a default whiteness covers the entire social space of LambdaMOO; race is whited out in the name of cybersocial hygiene.

Many Asian-American, African-American, and Latino users I interviewed commented on the reasons that they decide to exclude their "real life" race in their descriptions, and the consequences of their decisions. One player on LambdaMOO, a Korean-American woman, wrote:

> I never outright (in my desc) said I was Asian, because I felt that IRL [in real life] people already have stereotypes and felt that it would be at least as bad here, and I wanted to have a character that was free from that. Even before being experienced with net interactions, I pretty much feared what kind of people I would attract just by virtue of saying I'm an Asian woman. But then it bugs me that people just assume you're white if you don't say otherwise. Which is interesting because a lot of people here don't just assume you're heterosexual. They are careful to say SO instead of GF/BF and use [androgynous] pronouns or whatever.

She continued, "You know, though, people of color know exactly what it means to be limited in whatever way because they look the way they do. That is why, I'm sure people here don't take any pains to point out what they look like [. . .]." As this player explains, the few minorities on the Net are acutely aware of how their skin color "limits" them, and this—in conjunction with the informal "don't ask don't tell" policy of cyberspace—conspires to discourage minorities from presenting themselves *as* minorities.

The Berkeley Macintosh Users' Group, or BMUG for short, is a well-established community-based Internet bulletin board for Macintosh users, and it has an ethnically diverse membership. Players must use their real names and write résumés that any other player may read freely. After examining many of these, I noticed that users tended to describe their computers, their hair and eye color, their occupations, their pets—but race was very rarely mentioned. In this case of BMUG, a virtual space with strong ties to the University of California, Berkeley and progressive politics, the elision of race seems not to be motivated by fear of harassment or reprisal. Perhaps tolerance is so taken for granted there that users think that it doesn't need to be mentioned. Nonetheless, the effect is the same: if in cyberspace you are what you write, then the BMUGGERS, as they call themselves, have written race out too.

The dream of a new technology has always contained within it the fear of total control and the accompanying loss of individual autonomy. Perhaps the best way to subvert the hegemony of cybersocial hygiene is to use its own metaphors against itself. Racial and racist discourse in cyberspace are the unique products of machines and ideologies. Looking at discourse about race in cyberspace as a computer bug or ghost in the machine permits insight into the ways that it subverts that machine. A bug interrupts a program's regular commands and routines, causing it to behave unpredictably. "Bugs are mistakes, or unexpected occurrences, as opposed to things that are intentional" (Aker 12). Programmers routinely debug their work because they desire complete control over the way their program functions, just as Taffy and Nougat would like to debug LambdaMOO of its "sacrificial lambs," or those who insist on introducing new expressions of race into their world. Discourse about race in cyberspace is conceptualized as a bug, something an efficient computer user would eradicate since it contaminates her work/play. The unexpected occurrence of race has the potential, by its very unexpectedness, to sabotage the ideology-machine's routines. Therefore its articulation is critical, as is the ongoing examination of the dynamics of this articulation. Judith Butler writes,

> Doubtlessly crucial is the ability to wield the signs of subordinated identity in a public domain that constitutes its own homophobic and racist hegemonies through the erasure or domestication of culturally and politically constituted identities. And insofar as it is imperative that we insist upon those specificities in order to expose the fictions of an imperialist humanism that works through unmarked privilege, there remains the risk that we will make the articulation of ever more specified identities into the aim of political activism. Thus every insistence on identity must at some point lead to a taking stock of the constitutive exclusions that reconsolidate hegemonic power differentials [. . .]. (118)

The erasure and domestication of Asianness on LambdaMOO perpetuates an Orientalist myth of social control and order. As Cornel West puts it, "race matters," and as Judith Butler puts it, "bodies matter." Programming language and Internet connectivity have made it possible for people to interact without putting into play any bodies but those they write for themselves. The temporary divorce that cyberdiscourse grants the mind from the body and text from the body also separates race and the body. Player scripts that eschew repressive versions of the oriental in favor of critical rearticulations and recombinations of race, gender, and class, and which also call the fixedness of these categories into question, have the power to turn the theatricality characteristic of MOO space into a truly innovative form of play, rather than a tired reiteration of old hierarchies. Role-playing is a feature of the MOO—not a bug—and it would be absurd to ask that everyone who plays within it hew literally to their "real life" gender, race, or condition of life. A diversification of the roles that are permitted and played can enable a thought-provoking detachment of race from the body, and a questioning of the essentialness of race as a category. Performing alternative versions of self and race jams the ideology-machine, and facilitates a desirable opening up of what Butler calls "the difficult future terrain of community" in cyberspace (242).

GRAPHIC CHAT:
CYBERTYPING AND THE TYRANNY OF THE VISIBLE

According to Elizabeth Kolbert, in an article in the *New Yorker*, "Ultima Online, even with a quarter of a million subscribers, is two or three orders of magnitude larger than even the most populous MUD" (97). This is so despite the fact that MUDs and MOOs are free, while most graphic chat spaces charge monthly fees. It seems that most users strongly prefer to "see" who they're interacting with, even if they are aware that what they are "seeing" may bear no relation to the actual appearance of the user on the other end. Race becomes part of the visual language of graphic chat in a way that it could not be in textual chat, a factor that creates less difference than one might expect in terms of how race is dealt with in these spaces. Discourse about race is still elaborately "routed around," at least in terms of much interface design, avatar construction and deployment, and everyday discourse in Club Connect in spite of the fact that graphic avatars make race so visible. And even though the "club" is linked to an African American ethnic identity website, NetNoir, certain aspects of racial policing that obtain in LambdaMOO, albeit on an informal basis, are still in evidence at Club Connect.

My initial experiences with Club Connect did prove to inject race into graphic chat in ways that I had not seen in text-only environments and interfaces. The architects' dream of a multicultural virtual world is visible from the start. The log-on screen, which is the first thing that you see when you enter the website, features a little cartoon icon of a person's head, which greets you and asks you if you're having a problem with your password. Since it is practically guaranteed that most new users, especially ones who aren't computer-savvy, will have trouble with this step, viewers are given a great deal of exposure to this virtual greeter. The greeter is an icon of a fairly dark male with dreadlocks and African American features. Though it is generally a shaky move to make claims about which visual images look black, Asian, or in other ways "ethnic" since these judgments are always subjective and can tend to reduplicate the language of essentialism and racialism if not racism, this figure struck me as undeniably African American. This figure's position on this screen figures him as "tech support": both a servant of sorts and a technological expert. The figure paradoxically merges images of domestic laborers—like butlers and houseboys, images long associated with both blacks and Asians—and the computer geek figure, an image reserved for young white males. The figure looks young and "hip," as signified by the dreadlocks. These dreadlocks also gesture toward an ethnicity that is up front and center rather than elided or hidden, which is a real departure from the norm and a genuine innovation. (I can count the number of black icons I've seen on the Internet on *no* fingers.) This is a hopeful sign, particularly if one subscribes to the popular notion from media studies that models with color, images that "look like me," contribute to the inclusion of minorities offscreen as well.[6] Examining icons and avatars provides a wonderful occasion for an analysis of the principles of cybernetic iconography, a field that has yet to be born in relation to ethnic studies.[7] Analyzing the ways that icons and avatars are raced in cyberspace allows us to lay bare the principles of ethnic image-building on the Net that may seem transparent and "natural" to computer users, who are surrounded by icons every day. Thanks to Apple and Windows, icons are the matrix in which cyberspace users exist.

Once you've gotten past the password screen, Club Connect's software invites you to choose your gender, and then assigns you a "starter" or default body which you can further customize after getting acquainted with the site. The first time I logged on, I chose the gender "female" and was given the body and face of a young black woman, with fairly dark skin, African features, and short dark hair. I chose a name for my avatar, and began to explore the site. The first thing I noticed is that I was the only avatar among hundreds who was noticeably dark. While I saw many Asian-presenting female avatars, I saw no Asian-presenting male ones. This disparity can be accounted for, I am sure, by the fact that it isn't really a disparity: images of Asians in popular culture and the mainstream media do tend to be dominated by females, as in television newscasting, though this is slowly changing. On the other hand, I didn't see many strictly Anglo-presenting avatars, either. Many players chose light-skinned black female characters, Latino-presenting male characters, or Asian-presenting female characters, but there were relatively few black-presenting or Asian-presenting male characters.

I found other players to be extremely helpful and friendly. Perhaps this was because they could tell that I was a new player, but on a site this busy and populated, I suspect that their perceptions of me as "new" were conditioned by another factor. As I have mentioned earlier, I was the only truly dark character I could see anywhere. A friendly blond female, named mspiggy, offered to show me around, and when I expressed interest in exploring the ways I could customize my avatar, actually gave me a new head as a gift! This head, named "Rebecca," was one of dozens of models available via virtual vending machines that would take my virtual tokens and, in return, spit out a face for my avatar. Significantly, "Rebecca" was blonde and white-skinned; in fact, she greatly resembled my new online friend. While a great deal could be read into this psychologically, if one were so inclined, it seems to me indicative of the ways that beauty and race interact together in graphic chat spaces. Mspiggy's assumption that I would want a head that looked less "ethnic" seemed to project a particular image of beauty that was less, well, dark. Mspiggy showed me how to detach my old head, which I tucked under my arm, and helped me insert the new one. She then pointed out that my skin color and head color didn't match, saying "lol [laugh out loud] you look like you have a tan only on your arms!" and offered to help me to acquire some "body spray" so that I could change it. Throughout this exchange no mention of race was made.

Mspiggy led me to vending machines, where I viewed the multitude of different heads available to me. In an unconscious parody of cosmetic surgery and other technological image "enhancements," I noticed that these were priced across a wide range. I admit that I have not looked at every head available, but I did notice that none of them were as dark as my old one had been. This commodification of identity is reflected in the chat room's helpscreens on the topic of "changing and customizing your avatar's head," part of which reads,

Each head comes with its own default hair and face colors, which you may be able to customize. If custom face and hair colors are available, look for vending machines that sell or dispense head spray. If your head is sprayable, the popup menus of your avatar and the spray can will give you the necessary options for using the spray. Go ahead and experiment; you'll be able to change and adjust the colors again and again until you find the combination you like.

As hilarious as this description is, it seems to be doing more than simply pointing out the extent to which race has become elective in cyberspace; indeed, the passage omits any mention of race altogether. Instead of inviting you to give your avatar a race, just as you had given it a gender, the passage invites you to "experiment; you'll be able to change and adjust the colors again and again until you find the combination you like." Here, race is constructed as a matter of aesthetics, or finding the color that you like, rather than as a matter of ethnic identity or shared cultural referents. This fantasy of skin color divorced from politics, oppression, or racism seems to also celebrate it as infinitely changeable and customizable: as entirely elective as well as apolitical. Clearly, we must look to the subtextual, to the omitted and repressed, to find the place of race in graphic chat.

Implicit statements about race are to be found by looking at the relative pricing of heads, and the avatars of those around me. The marketplace and traffic in heads and bodyspray work in a traditional capitalistic system of supply and demand; that is to say, the types of heads for sale are available because there is demand for them: avatars are market-driven. If more players wanted to buy, for instance, extremely dark or Asian-looking male heads, undoubtedly they would have been on display, but they were not. The prevalent type seemed to be ethnically hybrid along particular lines: Asian-white females and light-skinned black females were quite popular. There were many male-presenting avatars with animal heads such as tigers, cats, and wolves—a fact in which a more inquiring mind than mine could undoubtedly find much meaning. Perhaps players choosing this option wished to defer the question of race permanently.

I did not try to ascertain the "real" racial identity of the other players on the site. In any case, the veracity of this information would always be in doubt, and it hardly seemed to matter, in a way. This conundrum, and a condundrum it is, reminded me of a similar one from literary studies: Does race reside in the author or in the text? It seems silly to say that a text like Maxine Hong Kingston's *Woman Warrior* should be discussed without any reference to the author's ethnicity and race. On the other hand, would that text not be just as "Asian" if we did not know the race and ethnicity of the author? In any case, I knew that many of the players had come from NetNoir's website, which was a good indication that many of them were African American, but since there are other ways to gain access to the site I knew also that many were not. The more interesting aspect of this whole thing seemed to be the question, When users are allowed to choose their races in graphic chat spaces, what do they choose? What do their choices say about the place of race in cyberspace? Why do they create the personae that they do? Where does race go when Asian-American and African-American users log on? Does it disappear?

As in text-only chat, the identities users choose say more about what they want than who they are, or rather, since these are eminently social spaces, what they think *others* want. In some sense, Club Connect is a racially diverse space, since players are choosing Asian- and African-American-presenting avatars, but since it is impossible to tell the race and ethnicity of these avatars offline, one must ask what kind of authenticity, integrity, or political efficacy these communities can have. The site's persistent avoidance of race as any kind of factor at all in the buying and selling of avatars that clearly *are* raced indicates a radical repression of what is all too often coded as a "divisive" subject, one to be avoided in the name of social harmony. However, like LambdaMOO, Club Connect displays a plethora of raced and gendered bodies, Asian and otherwise, that gesture toward a complex, multifaceted, and sometimes conflicted awareness of racial diversity. The notion that race can be customized, changed, and taken on or off as easily as one pops the head off a Barbie doll invokes the distinctive features of identity tourism. The metaphor of headhunting in cyberspace is a powerful one, since it also locates identity tourism in a matrix of colonial trophy-getting, a way of "eating the Other," to use bell hooks's phrase. Taming and framing the other by buying its signs and signifiers with virtual tokens seems indeed to be a form of virtual tourism, a kind of souvenir acquisition. The tyranny of visibility, of cybernetic "ways of seeing" in regard to race, has yet to be challenged in spaces like these.

MULTIPLY DISTRIBUTED IDENTITIES

The Net is, like other media, a reflection of the cultural imagination. It is a hybrid medium that is collectively authored, synchronous, interactive, and subject to constant revision. Because it borrows liberally from other media like television, film, and advertising, it is particularly sensitive to shifting figurations of race, and thus a good place to look to see how race is enacted and performed. I map sociologist Dean MacCannell's theories from *The Tourist: A New Theory of the Leisure Class* (1976) onto cybernetic racial role-players because I see many parallels. The tourist is also an explorer and navigator of sorts,[8] enjoying a recreational privilege reserved for "first world" leisure classes, just as do those who possess the material and cultural capital to gain access to the Net. The metaphor of travel that pervades the Net also evokes comparison with tourism, which offers no product but pure experience.[9] The most important point of comparison, though, is the relation between tourists and the "natives" that they see. Tourist desires for cultural authenticity, to encounter the other as they envision it, underpin their own sense of self as culturally authentic. Internet users who adopt other racialized personae can practice a form of tourism by adopting a repertoire of racial cybertypes. They replicate versions of otherness that confirm its exotic qualities and close off genuine dialogue with the pronounced minority of users who are not white and male.

The word *tourist* has a derisive connotation. MacCannell suggests that tourists are "reproached for being satisfied with superficial experiences of other people and places" (10). I use the term not to condemn those who pass as versions of the other, but rather because I wish to retain a sense of the identity tourist as one who engages in a superficial, reversible, recreational play at otherness, a person who is satisfied with an episodic experience as a racial minority. My fieldwork in role-playing spaces indicates that tourists desire experiences that they can legitimize as authentic. Their sojourns in the world of cyberspatial identity simulation through online role-playing are often used to confirm their ideas and underpin their ideal visions of the other. This passive version doesn't ask questions or challenge traditional stereotyped notions regarding its "nature." While gathering information for this project, I described myself as Japanese-American in my cybernetic self-portrait on LambdaMOO for a while, and for weeks until I edited it out of my description I was deluged with the same one-word message—*konmichiwa*, which means "hello" in Japanese. This vision of the Asian American as somehow *always* irremediably and stereotypically Asian, always knowing the language, and always receptive to the powers of one magical word that proves a type of cultural knowledge, conforms to touristic expectations about the unitarianism and nonhybridity of culture.

Multiply distributed identities allow identity tourists to simultaneously claim two positions, that of the tourist and that of the native; they can be both inside and outside.[10] If they never come across a samurai during their cybernetic travels, they can be one. Peopling the virtual landscape with samurai, homeboys, and sexy Latina women confirms a vision of ethnicity from which many in the offline world are struggling to distance themselves.[11] As actress and comedienne Margaret Cho said in an interview about how she was cast for the film *Fakin' the Funk*, "It's hard to be Asian-American and be castable. Your existence in the film must be justified. You cannot just be. You must be a computer expert, or a Kung Fu Master, or an exchange student, which is what I played." In cyberspace, as in film, the versions of race that most frequently get performed are those that are recognizable and familiar, hence heavily cybertyped: the logic of racial representation online makes it impossible to "just be," as Cho puts it, in most textual and graphic chat spaces.

In cyberspace, players do not ever need to look for jobs or housing, compete for classroom attention, or ask for raises. This ensures that identity tourists need never encounter situations in which exotic otherness could be a liability, an aspect of racial passing on the Internet that contributes to its superficiality. Players who represent as members of a minority may get the impression that minorities "don't have it all that bad," since they are unlikely to find themselves discriminated against in concrete, material ways. This imperfect understanding of the specific "real life" social context of otherness can lead to a type of complacency backed up by the seemingly unassailable evidence of "personal experience."

In Trinh T. Minh-ha's critique of anthropological methodology, *Woman Native Other*, she writes that "American tourists [. . .] looking for a change of scenery and pace in a foreign land [. . .] strike out in search of the 'real' Japan." For these tourists "authenticity [. . .] turns out to be a product that one can buy, arrange to one's liking, and/or preserve" (88). According to Trinh, tourists are searching for "the possibility of a difference, yet a difference or otherness that will not go so far as to question the foundation of their beings and makings" (88). Similarly, identity tourists perform a version of their ideal other that conforms to familiar stereotypes and does not ask questions or raise difficult, so-called divisive issues like racism: "No anthropological undertaking can ever open up the other. Never the marrow" (Trinh 73). The problem with believing that direct experience "as" the other will give access to knowledge about it, its marrow, is that this enterprise devalues actual conversation *with* it. There's a frisson about cultural transvestism that tantalizes identity tourists and makes them believe that, like Trinh's anthropologist, they can better understand the native through assuming a temporary alterity, by experiencing what they think "native" life is, rather than by acknowledging their reflexive position as an outsider, as other to the other. As Trinh asks, "[H]ow can he, indeed, read into the other knowing not how the other read into him?" Identity tourism is a type of nonreflexive relationship that actually widens the gap between the other and the one who only performs itself as the other in the medium of the cyberspace.

Bernard Gendron describes theories of the effect of technology on the human condition by dividing them into three categories: utopian, dystopian, and socialist (4–5). Observing racial and ethnic transvestism on the Internet leads me to conclusions that partake of all three of these categories. While the Net has great potential for expanding access to diversity and creating a globalistic point of view, it does not perform these functions as they exist today. The politics and economics of Net access, as well as the ways in which I

see race performed in role-playing spaces, leads me to conclude that
the advertising promises of Microsoft, IBM, and America Online to
"make the world smaller" are indeed being fulfilled in a disturbing
way. Perhaps opening up the Net through government subsidies
and infrastructure building in the schools will redress this problem,
but the incentives for minorities to opt for default whiteness online
will probably exist as long as there are material disadvantages to
nonwhiteness. Chat spaces, however nominally democratized they
may appear to be, are unlikely to eradicate these disadvantages.
The Net is a medium, a reflection of desires, fears, and anxieties
that exist in the culture, not a panacea for social ills and inequalities. The Internet is unlikely to lead to an apocalyptic breakdown of
literacy or morality, as some claim; rather, it is a laboratory where
users are building particular kinds of social environments
with words, as well as racialized personae to deploy within those
environments.

The personae choices that I see users making remind me of two
television shows that dramatize the position of the tourist in relation to other cultures. The first, *Fantasy Island*, exhibits a modern
sensibility and approach toward identity vacations; the second,
Quantum Leap, demonstrates a postmodern attitude which maps
nicely onto the phenomenon of identity tourism on the Internet. On
Fantasy Island, the tour guide impresario character, played by Ri-
cardo Montalbán, sells a very special kind of tour to privileged,
jaded Americans who want to temporarily experience life as race-
car drivers, movie stars, or action heroes. The stories of their experiences living lives radically different from their real lives are
usually given a cautionary twist; in a variation of the famous "Mon-
key's Paw" tale, fantasy vacationers usually realize that getting
one's fantasy is not as wonderful as it seems, and they leave the island with a newfound appreciation for what they had before. Being
another for a short while convinces the vacationers that they are really better off being themselves. The authenticity and integrity of
their real identities are never called into question; rather, they are
solidified and reinforced by their forays into role-playing.

Quantum Leap depicts a more disturbing variety of identity
switching. Sam Beckett, played by Scott Bakula, leaps from body to
body at different points in the historical continuum, assisted by a

computer-operating mentor (Al, played by Dean Stockwell) in his quest to right the racist and sexist wrongs of history. Sam, the embodiment of the late-twentieth-century white male consciousness, occupies such bodies as those of a black soldier in Vietnam, a pregnant teenager, and a black girl in the cross-burning South of civil rights protests. He can be anybody; he assumes these personae in the interest of keeping the historical continuum intact. He is the active, leaping agent of history, while the bodies (often of color) he occupies represent its passive, penetrable, and mute subjects, their Charley McCarthy to his Edgar Bergen. *Quantum Leap* is a tale about narrative transvestism with an important difference—in this narrative, technologically simulated identities controlled by a white male consciousness prove more powerful agents of history than those belonging to the less fortunate people who, unable to leap from period to period and body to body, must occupy them for life. Whereas on *Fantasy Island* all roads lead to home and a newfound appreciation of the self and its situation, Sam Beckett's home in *Quantum Leap* is the multiple personae that he inhabits. His subjectivity is distributed over multiple channels, just like a race-ethnicity-switching Internet user's subjectivity. This postmodern idea of the subject as a multiply distributed process rather than an essence challenges the idea of a core self that then assumes various masks—instead, the masks constitute the self. Read in terms of the Internet, this tale serves as a cautionary narrative about the power of technology to gift privileged subjects with a form of agency inaccessible to others.

The links between the history of media and the history of racial stereotyping are strong. The romantic, inaccurate, and sometimes overtly racist visions of the oriental that circulate in contemporary film, video games, television, and other electronic media are part of a vocabulary of signifying practices that are redeployed on the Internet by identity tourists. Role-playing on the Net and elsewhere are often characterized as games, and thus skeptics often claim that they bear no relation to the real world. Yet the specific ways in which Internet users choose to represent themselves online, the masks and personae of alterity that they fashion for themselves from images taken from the media landscape, reveal a great deal about their cultural and ideological investments and their assumptions about both the other and themselves. Racist ideology operates within role-playing spaces on the Net, creating a social matrix that is both "default white" and peopled with phantasmatic versions of otherness. To have any hope of approaching the utopian "level playing field" that so many claim is in the Internet's future, attention must be paid to *discourse with* rather than *appropriations of* the other.

< 3 >

RACE IN THE CONSTRUCT AND THE CONSTRUCTION OF RACE: THE "CONSENSUAL HALLUCINATION" OF MULTICULTURALISM IN THE FICTIONS OF CYBERSPACE

As has been shown in the case of online racial passing and identity tourism, users bring stereotyped notions of racial identity into cyberspace with them when they construct online personae. These images of race are often imported directly from popular media sources like films, video games, and novels. It is important to trace the intertextual links between these cybertypes and their source in genres like science fiction in order to observe the dynamics by which images are transcoded from older media to the new media of the Internet. Thus, a close reading of four canonical cyberpunk texts—two from the genre's beginnings in the 1980s (Ridley Scott's film *Blade Runner* and William Gibson's novel *Neuromancer*) and two from the 1990s (Neal Stephenson's novel *Snow Crash* and Andy and Larry Wachowski's film *The Matrix*)—can reveal the ways that these master narratives supply the specific imagery, tropes, and ways of representing race that provide the racial templates for online interactions. These narratives teach many users how to be raced in cyberspace. Cyberpunk has always had a particular investment in questions of embodiment and disembodiment as well as a preoccupation with hacker heroes who work outside official institutions of authority. The genre's emphasis on machine-enabled forms of consciousness seems to glorify, at times, the notion of the posthuman, which is also coded at times as the postracial. Despite this coding, however, race is all over cyberpunk's future terrains. Readers are presented with what looks like a postmodern multicultural future in these texts. This ostensible diversity is as much a "consensual hallucination" as is cyberspace itself, however, since these texts employ race as a means to stabilize the shaky boundaries of racial identity in the service of cultural coherence. As formerly solid notions of racial and ethnic identity are reconfigured and reenvisioned by a multitude of factors—specifically technology and the Internet—literary genres such as 1980s cyberpunk in particular attempt to shore them up by supplying the reader with racial cybertypes that are antique, nostalgic, and familiar. Second-generation nineties cyberpunk narratives like *Snow Crash* and *The Matrix* do this as well, but with a difference: they incorporate Asian "crossbreed" hero-protagonists as representatives of a distinctively new "ethnic group." Unlike *Blade Runner* and *Neuromancer*, which stick to the traditional casting formulas by featuring white actors and characters as centerpieces and orientalist and African figures as postmodern window dressing, these second-generation cyberpunk narratives turn that formula around to some extent by placing hybrid characters center stage and by focusing far more directly on racism, a political practice neglected by their precursors in the 1980s.

In the discourse of cyberpunk fiction and film, the future often looks bleak; though computer networks enable users to spend as much time outside of their bodies as in them and avail themselves of biotechnological enhancements like neural jacks, on-board weapons, and cosmetic surgeries, cyberscapes are dystopic: they are unremittingly gritty, urban, and plagued with unresolved social problems. While the genre of cyberpunk fiction has since expanded and been reiterated many times, one thing seems constant: when cyberpunk writers construct the future, it looks Asian—specifically, in many cases, Japanese. (I use the word *looks* for an important reason: while the future in *Blade Runner* and *Neuromancer* appears to *be* Japanese, this is in fact a visual trope rather than a meaningful reference to any real or imagined Japanese culture). Paradigmatic cyberpunk narratives like *Blade Runner*, William Gibson's *Sprawl* trilogy (of which *Neuromancer* is the first volume), and Neal Stephenson's *Snow Crash* all depict a seemingly multicultural "pan-Asian" future.

In *Blade Runner*'s Los Angeles, everyday life seems to have become infused with Japaneseness; sushi and udon have replaced hamburgers and burritos and Japanese has become a lingua franca; in the director's cut of the film, the first words spoken are in Japanese, as a Japanese food server queries the protagonist Deckard's order. Though Deckard refuses to answer in Japanese, he does understand it, and can argue with the food server on the basis of this shared knowledge, signifying the degree to which "Japan" has instantiated within itself cyberpunk's envisionings of a future Los Angeles. Indeed, the visual landscape of the film is decorated with enormous billboard-style images of geishas selling mysterious pills, and Japanese umbrellas, and the film is scored with Japanese-sounding music.

But how multicultural is this future? As other critics have noted, the film focuses on the predicament of the Tyrell corporation's replicants; as slaves they signify the disenfranchised, the forgotten and oppressed results of biotechnological hubris. The critical attention paid to their difference (from the human, from the "natural") has tended to obscure *other* differences within the film, however, such as racial ones. These replicants, hunted and reviled as they are, are constructed to be "perfect," as Tyrell's genetic designer J. R. Alexander notes, and it is no accident that they are all glamorous, athletic, and white.

Despite *Blade Runner*'s promiscuous and subsequently obligatory and conventional use of Asian imagery to "cyberfy" itself, the images of Asians and Asian culture that we see, all participate in specific types of stereotyped imagery. Geishas, greased paper umbrellas, and whiteface makeup all signify an antique Japanese past, preserved on film like a fly in amber and quoted in Ridley Scott's cyberfuture. Paradoxically, these anachronistic signs of Japaneseness are made, in the conventions of cyberpunk, to signify the future rather than the past.

Just as boundaries between the mind and the body are effaced or problematized by the "consensual hallucination" that is cyberspace, so too is the boundary between the past and the future mediated by images of Japanese geishas, ninjas, and samurai warriors. When these images are used to establish the distinctive look and feel of a cyberpunk future, the result is a high-tech variety of racial stereotyping: *techno-orientalism*. This term, which I have borrowed from Greta Niu, stresses the notion of new technologies used in the service of an old technology, that of creating a vision of Asia that is predictable, anachronistic, and reified as oriental. In Niu's words, "techno-orientalism [is]a way of viewing (of making an object of knowledge) Asian Americans without attending to the relationships between Asian bodies and technology" (2). *Blade Runner* beta-tested techno-orientalist imagery, so to speak, and its success as a canonical (*the* canonical) cyberpunk fiction legitimated its use for the genre it inaugurated.

While the film *Blade Runner* has been hailed as the "first cyberpunk narrative," the novel upon which it is based—Philip K. Dick's *Do Androids Dream of Electric Sheep?*—failed to garner the same kind of critical adulation. Perhaps this is because in Dick's novel, there is no detectable techno-orientalist imagery, no telegenic brew of seedy yet colorful Asian or multicultural visual elements. The orientalist imagery was retrofitted onto the novel by director Ridley Scott's film adaptation of the text. The influence of Scott's orientalist cybernarrative seems to have made techno-orientalism a required element or convention in much cyberpunk fiction since then, and it is certainly part of Gibson's *Neuromancer* which Bukatman writes heralded the "real advent of cyberpunk" (137). So it seems that orientalism has become part of this paradigm. (*Blade Runner* is cited as the first cyberpunk narrative despite the fact that it is a film and not a novel.) Indeed, in a 2001 article Gibson wrote for the *Observer*, he addresses this very issue head on: "Why has Japan been the setting for so much of my fiction? [. . .] Because Japan is the global imagination's default setting for the future" (n.p.). He goes on to ask again, "Why Japan, then? Because they live in the future, but neither yours nor mine, and somehow make it seem either interesting or comical or really interestingly dreadful." This claim that Japan is the "global imagination's default setting for the future" fails to acknowledge that Gibson's own fascination with Japan is partly the reason that it has come to signify the "future" in technological narratives. What's more, this future, which Gibson is careful to cordon off as permanently other in relation to the West (it is "neither yours nor mine"), must be cybertyped with traditional signifiers of the oriental.

Ridley Scott has also had an ongoing fascination with Japan in his films made in the eighties, such as *Black Rain*. (The eighties were also the heyday of cyberpunk as a genre: Bruce Sterling identifies cyberpunk as the product of "technosocial changes loose in contemporary society" in the eighties [40].) *Black Rain* works through American anxiety about multinational corporate competition from Japan and, by extension, multiculturalism. Fears that Japan's dominance of high-tech industries such as electronics manufacture would imperil the U.S. economy drive the plot, and, most importantly, situate Japan as both antique and authentic (as in the film's kendo-playing scenario) yet futuristic: as in Gibson's Japan fictions, it is that future that is "neither yours nor mine." Similarly, *Neuromancer* sets up its American white hacker protagonist, Case, as a warrior against Japanese capitalism: he is a data thief who steals from zaibatsus, the cyberpunk model of capitalism in the future: "Power, in Case's world, meant corporate power. The zaibatsus, the multinationals that shaped the course of human history, had transcended old barriers. Viewed as organisms, they had attained a kind of immortality" (203). Many critics, such as David Brande, have discussed the ways in which Gibson critiques and refigures capitalism, yet none seem to discuss the racial politics or historical context of that critique as a product of 1980s American Japanophobia.

While *Blade Runner* and *Neuromancer* appear to be multicultural, their lack of main or even less than peripheral characters who are nonwhite signals the limitations of cyberpunk as a genre when it comes to representing ethnic and racial diversity in meaningful ways.[1] The dearth of Asian protagonists represents a step forward (or step backward?) in orientalist stereotyping in popular media.

When the body gets complicated and problematic, so does personal identity. *Racial* identity must be policed and solidified in cyberpunk narrative in order to compensate for wobbly boundaries between the mind and the body. On a related note, the students in my world and postcolonial literature courses are of the opinion that in the future, race will disappear, and that everyone will be mixed. They say this in a matter-of-fact way, not at all as if it is a bad thing, yet at the same time they're very interested in ethnic identity—especially their own—and believe that people ought to both acknowledge and celebrate their ethnic heritage, rather than neglect or ignore it. This paradox is one I've pushed them to examine.

Their vision of the future as raceless, irremediably hybrid to the point where racial definition becomes an exercise in futility, is strongly resisted in cyberpunk fiction. This resistance comes at a time when "the dizzying uncertainty over the best way to count people who list themselves as more than one race points out two of the starkest facts now emerging about America's racial and ethnic profile; never have Americans been so diverse; never have they been so confused" (Holmes 1). Radical ambiguity regarding the best way to describe an increasingly racially and ethnically hybrid American population gives rise to a confusion that is laid to rest in these fictions by asserting the solidity of solid, old-fashioned, cybertyped notions of race. Holmes goes on to write that "the expansion of the racial categories [made available on the U.S. Census—recently the categories were expanded in number from 5 to 63] and the sharp increase during the 1990s in the number of Hispanics, who can be of any race, has scrambled the racial landscape" (1).

This "scrambled racial landscape" gets unscrambled in cyberspace and its fictions; the desire to stabilize radically shifting conceptual ground and shore it up is addressed through cybertyping. Fears that race will disappear in the future through intermarriage and interbreeding are calmed by persistent visions of the orient as still solidly there—more antique, exotic, and oriental than ever. When the meat gets left behind, in theory so does race, but these 1980s cyberpunk narratives have so much invested in the idea of their white heroes as *American* underdogs that they must keep racial boundaries intact.

Asians function in these texts as enablers for white console cowboys to move their narratives forward; they're mediators between the machine and the body in *Neuromancer* (the Chinese black medic Gerald Chin who does Molly's various cybernetic bodily implants, the creators of the Hosaka and Ono-Sendai cyberspace decks, and Chiba City's nerve splicers are all examples of Asian cyborg body-science). These Asian characters install, manufacture, and maintain the body modifications that make heavy duty hacking possible for console cowboys. While the white male cowboys in *Neuromancer* duel it out in cyberspace, using their minds like weapons, the Asian characters supply the props but stay hidden in the wings; there are no Asian hackers in this novel. They act as the

Tonto to the hacker's Lone Ranger: as Toni Morrison writes regarding the narrative function of blacks in American literature, "cooperative or sullen, they are Tontos all, whose role is to do everything possible to serve the Lone Ranger without disturbing his indulgent delusion that he is indeed alone" (82). The Asian characters' presence here as racial foils highlights the notion that race *must* continue to exist, especially in the terrain of cyberspace, where so many foundational notions of identity as anchored in a body have become contingent, problematic, and difficult.

Case, the outlaw-hacker protagonist in *Neuromancer*, deploys his consciousness in cyberspace as a way of hacking out his living, but more importantly, as a means of escaping the "meat," the condition of being in a body he experiences as constraining. *Cyberspace* (a term coined by Gibson in this novel and subsequently picked up by computer scientists) is *about* disembodiment in a fundamental sense: the hacker's mind in the matrix represents a pure Cartesian cogito that detaches qualities of identity from the physical body. A "flipflop switch" enables Case to experience the "sensorium" of Molly, the "razorgirl" whose consciousness he inhabits through the medium of his Japanese-made cyberspace deck. This ability to switch genders, this interrogation of gender as a detachable quality that can be "flipflopped" in the matrix of disembodiment that is cyberspace, does not however translate to a corresponding interrogation of race. It is as if the dammed-up anxieties of disembodiment that might lead to such inconvenient questions as whether anybody is really "white" or "Asian" or whether such categories meaningfully exist must be contained by shoring up a solid notion of *race* as a bodily quality.

Cyberspace and race have at least one important thing in common: both are consensual hallucinations. As Anthony Appiah notes,

in a society like ours, where most people take their race to be a significant aspect of their identity, it comes as a shock to many to learn that there is a fairly widespread consensus in the sciences of biology and anthropology that the word "race" at least as it is used in most scientific discussions, refers to nothing that science should recognize as real. (277)

Appiah's reference to science's role in defining race reveals much about how knowledge is constructed, and the ideological uses to which essential categories such as race, which has been persistently misunderstood as a biological quality, have been put. It seems no accident that just as the human sciences, such as biology and anthropology, are debunking the notion of race as a meaningful biological term, and the computer sciences are challenging our senses of ourselves as unproblematically ensconced in bodies that possess genders and races, the fictions of cyberpunk are rebunking or reinforcing the notion of race as an essential category. There are pressing ideological reasons for it to do so.

As cyberspace begins to challenge our sense of space as conditioned by distance and time (e-mail is instant, telecommunications give the sense of simultaneity and presence), borders get muddled—most notably borders relating to nationality and ethnicity. The utopian, McLuhanesque notion of a "global village" enabled by cybertechnology gets reinscribed in Gibson's work as the sinister Japanese zaibatsu, whose multifarious and hegemonic presence on the Net conditions all flows of social power and capital. The only thing protecting American democracy and individualism from total destruction by the rhizomatic "evil empire" of orientalist commerce is the lone hacker. In order for this representative of the Western frontier and way of life, the cowboy, to police and reform muddled borders and reclaim America from the zaibatsus, he must be presented to us as unproblematically white. Hence, the ubiquity of the oriental foil and orientalia in general in fiction of this kind. These remind us of the persistence of racial difference: they serve to police the border that threatens to muddle racial categories and thus take disembodiment to its logical conclusion: if there is no body, there can be no race in the biological sense. That is, race must then be understood as a function of consciousness rather than something that is visible and written on the body.

In addition, these fictions address a related technological phenomenon that comes with its own anxieties: plastic surgery. Elective surgeries are a convention in most cyberpunk fictions: body modifications are a twist on the already-present theme of disembodiment, or the body called into question. In *Neuromancer*, adolescents such as the prankster-hacker Panther Moderns elect to acquire epican-

thic folds. This is a reversal of the present order of things, in which
most surgeries involving epicanthic folds have to do with removing
them. It gestures toward a world in which some of the physical
markers of race and ethnicity continue to be commodified, but in
particularly Eurocentric ways.

Oriental warriors and their eyelids function as commodities in
Neuromancer; in a world gone artificial they represent the natural,
the authentic, the rare, the exotic. The presence of Hideo, the
Tessier-Ashpool family's ninja, seems anomalous and asynchronous,
and gestures toward a "real" Japanese past that, by contrast, makes
the futureworld of cyberpunk that much more futuristic. Hideo is
described as "a small man, Japanese, enormously polite, who bore
all the marks of a vatgrown ninja assassin. Smith sat very still, star-
ing into the calm brown eyes of death across a polished table of
Vietnamese rosewood" (74). This corny, cliché-ridden description
of the Asian warrior, with his "calm brown eyes of death," identifies
him metonymically with the polished table of rare Vietnamese rosewood, another status symbol and commodity of a rich family. Both
serve to stabilize the embattled lines between the natural and the
"vatgrown," the futuristic and the nostalgic. Gibson's use of this
type of language distinctively invokes a dark, humorless, sublime,
orientalist world. And, like anchovies, this is either loved or hated
by the readers.

While first generation cyberpunk texts hold racial and ethnic
hybridity at bay by asserting the solidity of orientalist cybertypes,
second-generation texts such as *Snow Crash* and *The Matrix* acknowledge racial hybridity, even if at times this acknowledgment is
covert. Despite this widening of the conceptual circle to include
more complex formulations of race, these texts still rely upon a system of racial cybertyping in which kung fu, jujitsu, samurai swords,
and other orientalist signifiers work to let us know that we are in
the future. On the other hand, these narratives do depict racism in
this future, and also, importantly, feature African-American and
Asian-American characters as more than just window dressing.[2]

Neal Stephenson's 1995 novel *Snow Crash* parodies and mocks
just about every convention of cyberpunk fiction established by
Gibson, including Gibson's use of techno-orientalism; Stephenson's
novel, deemed part of the "second generation" of the cyberpunk

genre (Porush 110) shows a future world that still looks Asian, and
thus conforms to the convention set by Gibson and Scott, but it
looks distinctly *Pan*-Asian, with equal references to Chinese, Aleut-
ian, Korean, and Japanese cultures.

Stephenson's particular brand of techno-orientalism is distinctively different from Gibson's and Scott's. *Snow Crash*'s protagonist, Hiro Protagonist, is a "solitary crossbreed with a slick custom
avatar who's packing a couple of swords" and wearing a black
leather kimono. He has "eyes which look Asian. They are from his
mother, who is Korean by way of Nippon. The rest of him looks
more like his father, who was African by way of Texas by way of the
Army" (20). His "cappuccino skin and spiky, truncated dreadlocks"
signify his place both on the margins of legitimate business—always
the position of choice for the hacker/rocker/cyberpunk hero/Hiro—
and his position as a multiply raced subject. He is both the orientalist samurai figure reprised in Gibson's *Neuromancer* as Hideo, and
a dreadlocked, slick, black-leather-clad African-American urban-
ite. This kind of hero protagonist is raced quite differently from
Neuromancer's Case, who is "default white" since he seems to lack
ethnic or racial roots or referents of any kind. Thus, Stephenson is
able to convey a more complicated kind of racial hybridity than is
expressible in "first-generation" cyberpunk narratives, while at the
same time retaining the exotic Orientalism which is so strongly
identified with it. This signifies that techno-orientalism is a robust
enough feature of the genre that it could not be discarded. Like
Hiro himself, the novel keeps a foot in two worlds: one in the world
of first-generation cyberpunk, and one in more contemporary "real
world" of the 1990s, where ethnicity and race are in the process of
being actively reconfigured.

In *The Diamond Age* Stephenson's on-going parody of first-generation cyberpunk reinvisions *Neuromancer*'s sinister corporate zaibatsu as the "FOQNE," or "franchise-organized quasi-national
entity." These FOQNEs, which include "signatory tribes, phyles,
registered diasporas, and sovereign polities," have replaced nation-
states as purveyors of ethnic identity. In Mr. Lee's Greater Hong
Kong, as in the Cosa Nostra's Nova Siciliana, a sign is prominently
posted which proclaims the FOQNE's philosophy:

the potentials of all ethnic races and anthropology to merge
under a banner of the Three Principles to follow:

1. Information, information, information!
2. Totally fair marketeering!
3. Strict ecology. (*SC* 99)

Mr. Lee's philosophy seeks to transcend race as well by adhering to
a libertarian-style intensely capitalist set of "Three Principles" as
listed on this sign. This goes along with Stephenson's penchant for
describing all sorts of subcultures as "new ethnic groups." In *Snow
Crash* he notes that in the Metaverse there were enough avatars of
"Clints and Brandies to form a new ethnic group" (*SC* 37) and
comments on the "longtime status of skateboarders as an oppressed
ethnic group" (*SC* 77), and in *The Diamond Age* calls the Mouse
Army of orphaned Chinese girls "a new ethnic group of sorts" (*DA*
446).[3] Clearly, part of the excitement of Stephenson's future world
lies in its creation of new configurations of ethnicity, one that
prefers, in these instances at least, to avoid overt references to race.

This is not to say, however, that racism doesn't exist in this future. Unlike Gibson, Stephenson makes several overt references to
old-fashioned racism, establishing beyond a doubt a vision that es-
chews the sublime tone of *Neuromancer*'s stylistics for a more realis-
tic and biting commentary on how racial and ethnic groups work
under global capitalism. For example, the Apartheid Burbclaves,
walled communities featuring signs that read "WHITE PEOPLE
ONLY. ALL NON-CAUCASIANS MUST BE PROCESSED" (*SC* 32)
attest to the ongoing existence—indeed, the commodification—of
race-based border patrolling on private as well as public property.
This is most emphatically *not* the world without borders celebrated
in much contemporary advertising for the Internet: *la frontera* is still
policed, albeit by private security firms rather than the Immigration
and Naturalization Service. Even though one can self-present as any
kind of avatar (hence, any kind of race) one wishes in the Metaverse,
(within the limits of programming ability or economic means, since
avatars can be either bought or made for the user) Stephenson does
not then make the leap that some of the Internet's early utopian
boosters did—that is to say, he does not assume that because race

can be hidden online racism cannot exist there. Indeed, Hiro's encounter in the Metaverse with a racist Japanese businessman who challenges Hiro's right as part African-American to carry his father's samurai swords works to assure the reader that despite the deconstruction (or rather corporatization) of ethnic identity in the post-Internet world, racism is as robustly ongoing a feature of postmodern life as cyberspace is. In addition, this incident reminds us that despite Hiro's function as a referent to the orientalist-ninja-warrior paradigm evident from the earliest cyberpunk narratives, he no more belongs in the world of Nippon than he does anywhere else; his dark skin and spiky dreadlocks make that a certainty. Stephenson represents him as a "new ethnic group" unto himself: a "solitary crossbreed." In a similar move, the Wachowski brothers' 1999 film *The Matrix* also features a racially hybrid hero, played by Keanu Reeves, who is surrounded by a matrix of orientalist cyberpunk trappings. However, this film's more intense engagement with racism in a machine-dominated future distinguishes it both from *Snow Crash* and from earlier cyberpunk fictions.

> MORPHEUS: The Matrix is a world pulled over your eyes to blind you from the truth.
> NEO: What truth?
> MORPHEUS: That you are a slave, Neo. Like everyone else, you were born into bondage.

This dialogue occurs in *The Matrix*, and through it Morpheus reveals that Neo has been living in a dreamworld created by a sinister artificial intelligence that has reduced humans to organic power sources to fuel their own processors and, most importantly, has constructed a digital representation of the "real world" so convincing that most humans assume it to be real. This matrix, or "neural-interactive simulation," is a digital construct indistinguishable from the real. The danger lies in the exploitation of the human race, at least those of it still enslaved by its simulated reality. The connections between the matrix as depicted in this film and the Internet as it exists today all have a common root in cyberpunk fiction, specifically William Gibson's novels. Gibson was the first to apply the term *matrix* to technology to describe a network of computers that had achieved sentience: he coined the word *cyberspace* as a means to describe a "consensual hallucination experienced daily by billions of legitimate operators" (51). Hence, the film *The Matrix* can (and should) be read as a narrative about the Internet and its possibilities and dangers.

Like Gibson's novels in particular and cyberpunk in general, *The Matrix* both celebrates and critiques technology. The cyberutopian or celebratory strain often advances the notion of technology as a social equalizer that levels out race and gender inequities, since bodies are supposedly left behind in cyberspace, or at least are invisible when one is using it. This line of thinking depends upon a mistaken notion of race as solely a somatic or bodily feature, one that can (and should) be conveniently edited out or eliminated through the use of the Internet. *The Matrix* is all about visibility, however, and thus cannot elide the question of race (though at times it tries to, with important repercussions, as I will show). On the contrary, I posit that the film envisions a vexed multiculturalism as a corrective to the dehumanizing excesses of modern machines, which promise so much but end up delivering so little.

Though the film has been called "equal parts Luddite polemic and seeker of truth" (Anthony, n.p.) its "truth" couches a critique of technology within a deeply raced narrative. In this narrative, humans must learn to master machines, not abandon them. Race functions as a means for humans to hack into the machines; it represents a "pirate signal" that affirms racial diversity and stakes out its place in the global landscape of the future. Utopia (or "Zion," as it is termed in the film) is the last refuge of "100 percent pure homegrown human beings," as the black character Tank terms himself. This future world is emphatically multiracial; rather than a place in which race has been "transcended" or represented solely by white actors (who command more money at the box office) we are shown a world in which race is not only visible but necessary for human liberation.

Neo's dialogue with Morpheus, one of many that contribute toward the orientalized sensei/student relationship they share, employs a term that cannot ever be separated from power relations and race in the United States—that is, *slavery*. Morpheus's efforts to school Neo, to first convince him that he is a slave exploited by machine culture and later to help him to "free his mind" so that he can defeat the machines and rewrite, or hack into, the matrix, reverses the usual order of things in a film of this genre. Firstly, it constructs a black character as a leader in a cyberpunk film, and in fact as more than a leader; as the character Tank says while delivering an elegy to Morpheus, who he thinks will be shortly unplugged or killed, "You've been more than a leader to us, you've been a father." Previous canonical cyberpunk films have depicted minority characters, particularly Asians, as window dressing symptomatic of a postapocalyptic pastiche of cultures; in *Blade Runner* (1982), the viewer can tell that the apocalypse has come and gone because there are so many minorities running around speaking in foreign languages, or mixtures thereof. The same can be said of *Strange Days* (1995). In both of these films, people of color are supporting characters at best.

In noticeable contrast, *The Matrix* comes closer to being a truly multicultural cyberpunk film; perhaps this, in part, has had something to do with this film's "regenerating the sagging cyberspace genre" (Croal 64), a genre that had been "left-for-dead," in the words of a *Newsweek* review.[4] However, though the review refers to the "combination of Chinese martial arts and American special effects" that have created the spectacular hybrid fight scenes that most filmgoers remember, it says nothing about race and the casting of the film, much less the ways that race is constantly referenced in the narrative. It seems as if the film's critical reception exists in another matrix or frame of reference—one in which race is invisible, overshadowed by the conflict between men and machines. Since the film's release, however, the role of race in casting decisions has been publically acknowledged by Jada Pinkett, an African-American actress who had been considered for the female lead in *The Matrix*. As she noted in an interview "'[W]hen Val dropped out and Laurence [Fishburne] came in, it was sort of like, 'There's only going to be one black person in this film [. . .]. But I believe things happen for a reason. Carrie-Anne [Moss] kicked ass in that movie, and now it's come back around to me'" (DeVries 124). According to Pinkett, it appears that the filmmakers wanted some "color" in the movie, but wanted to avoid making it "too black" by having more than one African-American leading character. With the exception of

Pinkett's statement, the delicate balance struck between racial types in the film has been generally ignored in favor of a focus on another sort of difference, that between humans and machines. However, in the film, machines are raced and so are men (women are another story). A black man leads the resistance or slave revolt against the machines, who are visible to us as Anglo-Saxon "agents" wearing suits.[5] They all look the same, as one would expect machines to do, but most importantly they all look white and middle class in a way that no one in the resistance does.

The black Morpheus is a "father" to his multicultural crew of rebels, which is impressive in its diversity: in addition to Morpheus, it contains two black characters, Tank and Dozer, an adolescent white boy, Mouse, a Latino figure, Apoc, and a white woman, Trinity. There is even a queer female character, Switch, signified as such by familiar tropes such as spiky hair, minimal makeup, and a matter-of-fact way of speaking; but her queerness isn't flagged by the characters pointing it out via dialogue, just as race isn't constructed in that way either (it being taken for granted that by 2199, the year when the "real" action is taking place, racial diversity as well as tolerance vis-à-vis sexual identity has become accepted enough to go without comment). The discourse of racism has been repurposed in this film, however. At times it is projected onto machines, as when Morpheus is beaten and abducted by the white agents; his reply to learning Agent Smith's name is "You all look the same to me." Primarily, the presence of people of color in the film lets us know that we are in the realm of the *real:*[6] machine-induced fantasies and wish fulfillments, which is what the matrix is, are knowable to us by their distinctive and consistent whiteness.

The machine in its worst incarnation—the sinister face of technology run amok, the hegemonic, cyberspatial, cold regime that has reduced all humans to slaves—is shown to us in the film as being distinctively and conventionally *white and male*, in contrast to the warm, living multiraciality and gender-bending of the rebels. The agents are the visual manifestation of a system of domination that is technologically enabled, and they appear in suits which signify a critique of corporate imagery in general as well as "capitalism as usual." The agents also manifest themselves as cops, clearly allied with the hegemonic machine, and the scene in which they gather in

a circle and beat the black Morpheus invokes images of the Los
Angeles beating of Rodney King, images indelibly coded as being
about the oppression of blacks by whites.

The only four white characters in the crew, the warrior-heroine
Trinity, the androgynous Switch, the hacker-boy Mouse, and the be-
trayer Cypher, are positioned either in opposition to or in alliance
with this version of whiteness; Cypher, the only white man on the
crew, is on the side of the machines; he is their agent. Mouse, as well
as Switch, the queer female character, and Trinity, the other female
crew member, are emphatically against the machines. Both Switch
and Trinity, in particular, unite a cyberpunk style of femininity and
a formidable role as a warrior; Trinity's is the first combat scene in
the film.[7] Trinity and Switch stand outside traditional gender definitions of woman as nurturer and victim in need of defending. While
the machine defends traditional gender roles—there are no female
agents—Trinity and Switch challenge them, which exempts them
from the taint of whiteness-as-inhuman and preserves femininity as
an opposing force to technology as oppressor. This race constructing
of the machine itself identifies whiteness as part of the problem, not
the solution, a problem that multiraciality—the alliance between
blacks, as shown to us by Morpheus, Tank, and Dozer, Latinos like
Apoc, and interracial characters like Neo—is positioned to solve.

The multiracial position of Neo, played by Keanu Reeves, is oc-
cluded to some extent in the film. However, it is a significant casting choice to have placed him in this role precisely because of his
mixed racial status. Early journalistic writing on Keanu Reeves often took note of his mixed Asian and white heritage. Significantly,
the decision was made in 1999—the same year as the film's release—to make the choice "Other" available in the race category of
the U.S. Census. This official recognition that people who don't fit
into one racial "box" do exist in demographically significant numbers represents a significant paradigm shift in our national conceptions of race, one that this film recognizes by making a character of
mixed race its hero, literally "the one"—humanity's only hope
against oppressive whiteness and the enslavement and eventual
eradication of humanity that whiteness represents in the film.

Neo unites within himself the rainbow of races that have come
to stand for "the human" in the film; like the stunning special effect

termed "recursive action," or as John Gaeta, the effects coordinator of the film calls it, "the fist bouquet." Keanu makes visible all the different varieties of color including white; his hybridity is marked as the only available corrective to the agents of whiteness. Machines take on the onus that previously belonged to racial others and unite nonwhite men and white women against a system or matrix of white purity and privilege as exemplified by institutions such as the law and corporations—specifically high-tech corporations. Here the film's critique of information technologies and their alliance with capitalism is particularly apparent; the company that Neo works for, Metronex, is staffed almost entirely with white men, as is the digital Construct, which is part of the rebels' training program.

The idea that all whites are, to some extent, unwittingly or not "agents" of the racism machine relates to George Lipsitz's notion of the "possessive investment in whiteness" (vii). In his book of the same name, Lipsitz explains the dynamics by which whites often unknowingly consent to the perpetuation of their own entitlements and privilege in relation to nonwhites. Lipsitz is careful to note that not all whites participate in this system, that indeed many whites have resisted it strongly and continue to do so, but the fact that there is an array of ready-made institutions or machinic systems designed to produce white privilege provides them with that choice, a choice lacking for nonwhites. The fact that the possessive investment in whiteness is often unconscious gestures toward the nature of racism in the age of multiraciality and multiculturalism, a time when claiming such privilege overtly classes one in a socially undesirable category, that of white supremacist or racist. As Morpheus says of the business-suited whites peopling the Construct, these "plugged in" people think they are living in the real world, but instead are experiencing a hallucination, and thereby have been made "so helplessly inert, so dependent on the system, they will fight to protect it." It is not possible to "liberate" such humans; like the majority of whites as described in Lipsitz's work, they are dependent on the system of privilege that allows them to be on the winning side of Information-Age capitalism and the machines that underpin it. To unplug them from their dream of whiteness and its attendant comfort would be to kill them. This may explain the lack of white men among the Rebels: theoretically, nonwhites and women are the ones who would *want* to wake up from this particular dream.

Cypher, the only white man on the crew, betrays the humans precisely because he wants to jump the ship of multiculturalism and reclaim his possessive investment in whiteness.[8] He negotiates with Agent Smith, who addresses him as Mr. Reagan—a fine jab at the trickle-down capitalism of the 1980s that perpetuated white privilege—to be "replugged" into the system, where he can eat steak and drink red wine in a fine restaurant. The fact that he knows that this privilege is an illusion—the steak and wine are digital simulations provided by the agents—and that he must kill his crewmates to get it signifies the ways in which the virtual have colonized the real, to the detriment of the real, and most importantly, the ways in which white maleness are always constructed as suspect in the film. In the scene where he kills Apoc, Switch, and Dozer and almost kills Tank, Cypher relates that his grievances have specifically to do with the *lack* of privilege and entitlements he feels in the real world; he cries, "I'm tired of this ship, tired of being cold, tired of eating the same goddam glop every day."

He wants to be the "one," feels *entitled* to be the one, but the multicultural logic of the film will not allow it; in order for the critique of whiteness to be completed he must be the Lu(Cypher) of the story and his white hubris must be punished by death. Indeed, his claims to be oppressed while he is receiving no less and no more than any other crew member—we are pointedly shown that everyone eats the same glop, which issues from a tube in the ship—invokes the ways that a lack of white privilege can be experienced as oppression. Lipsitz notes the case of Allan Bakke, a white man who successfully sued the University of California for "reverse discrimination,"and the ways that it mobilized protest against affirmative action; in it the "language of liberal individualism serves as a cover for collective group interests" (22)—in this case the interests of whites. In the digital video disc version of the film, this section is entitled "Dealing for Bliss," a title that takes note of the "deals" that whites can make, with themselves (i.e., denial or incomprehension that a deal has even taken place) and with the institutions and practices that underpin racism.

The Matrix constructs a new discourse of race in the Digital

Age, one that plugs us in to our own dreamworlds about cy-
berutopias and cyberfutures. And like any dream, it is conflicted: it
opens a window into our cultural anxieties, fears, fantasies, and desires about the Internet and the roles of blacks, whites, machines,
and all combinations thereof. Like the Internet, the matrix looks
the way we want it to look or have made it look: it is symptomatic
of our vision of utopia. It is a construct, a wonderland of sorts, as
the film's frequent reference to Lewis Carroll's *Alice in Wonderland*
broadly signals. As Morpheus says to Neo about the matrix, "Your
mind makes it real."

Indeed, cyberspace engenders particular questions about what is
"real," and the implications of these questions are increasingly unavoidable today: as pundits of digital culture debate such problems
as the "reality" of online relationships, chat-room identities, and
the status of the self on the Internet, we are faced with a radical interrogation of the nature of personal identity. Millions of users create online identities via e-mail, chat rooms, and web construction
that may vary quite a bit from their "real life" identities. This signifies the desire for elasticity in identity construction: it gestures toward a sense that we are more than we appear, or wish to be read
differently than we are, and can use cyberspace to create versions of
ourselves that look and in some sense are different from ourselves.
Much research has been done on this phenomenon of gender (and
to a much less extent racial) cross-dressing or masquerade on the
Internet, and the jury is still out on whether this should be viewed
as a progressive aspect, one that liberates users and encourages
democratic social relations, or whether it simply reduplicates old
gender and race hierarchies.[9] The matrix is an embodied cyberspace, meaning that in order to be there you have to have a body,
albeit a digital body. This body, which is created by the mind, is
known in cyberspace literature as an avatar.[10] The avatar is described by Morpheus to Neo as "residual self-image [. . .] it is the
mental projection of your digital self."

Thus, while the "real" Neo is wearing a tattered sweater, his
head is shaved, his skin is pale and unhealthy looking, and his body
still bears the marks of the plugs and ports that connected him to
the sinister machines, the Neo-in-cyberspace has coifed hair, stylish
black clothing, and looks as glamorous as only Hollywood lighting

and excellent makeup can make him look. Indeed, *all* of the rebels undergo this transformation while they are in the matrix fighting the agents; they wear full-length leather coats, natty Prada-ish suits, painfully stylish haircuts, cyberpunk mirrorshades, and high-tech PVC fabrics and silks.[11]

This transformation, like the changes in self-presentation that Internet users execute when they create a visual "self" to deploy in cyberspace, says a great deal more about what users *want* than who users *are*. Or rather, in cyberspace it boils down to the same thing. The striking aspect of the way the matrix's avatars look has to do with the solidity of race. Avatars can look any way you want them to: they are aspects of "residual self-image." This term *residual* seems to signify that the mind "re-members" the body only partially; when it constructs itself in the matrix, aspects of it are left out. Race is part of this residue; it is that which the mind identifies as belonging to itself, an essential and indispensable part of itself. Hence, none of the characters are differently raced when in the matrix. Instead, they create versions of themselves that are differently classed: glossier, better dressed, more powerful. They upgrade themselves and the accouterments of class identity: their clothes, their abilities, their hair (lots of hair gel in the matrix), their weapons and cars—but their race stays the same throughout. In a world where you can download special abilities, such as kung fu, jujitsu, and the ability to fly a B-212 helicopter, knowledge is a fluid thing, yet race remains solid; it is inseparably part of the self in a way that mere class cannot be.

However, in contemporary Internet practice, users change their gender and race all the time. Why does the film leave this more radical and highly publicized (stories about men on the Net who really turn out to be women are fodder for talk shows) transformation out of the picture? While the critique of whiteness and machines together seems to affirm multiculturalism and hybridity as correctives to the alienation and exploitation of most humans today, the film passes up a prime opportunity to question the monolithic nature of race more radically. Race is not a fluid in this film, but a solid in the sense that while hackers into the matrix can change just about any aspect of themselves, they cannot (or significantly do not choose to) change their race.

I read this move as an affirmation that race matters: racial diversity is depicted as a source of the heroes' strength. (And of course there is the matter of movie stars needing to get their proper amount of screen time. Since Keanu Reeves's name is above the title on the promotional material, we can expect that filmgoers' expectations to see him on film most of the time must be indulged.) Non-whiteness is what makes the "real" humans different from the artificial agents. Race serves to anchor the viewer in the "real," a crucial function in a film that sets out to bend viewers' minds regarding the status of the real,[12] a status that is changing at a vertiginous rate in our world as well.

Neo's nausea and vomiting when he discovers that what he thought was the "real" him is simply a version or digital avatar of him signifies the sense of nausea that goes along with rapid and unexpected movement. Vertiginous shifts in cultural, physical/ontological, and epistemological points of view are engendered by digital identity switching; in a sense Neo's nausea mirrors our own in the face of radical instability regarding personal identity. Race in general and blackness in particular stabilize this cybervertigo of identity: as Neo wakes from his pod-induced trance, his first sight in the "real world" is the face of a black man, Morpheus. The first words that Neo hears as a "real person" are "Welcome to the real world." These particular words, coming as they do from Laurence Fishburne's character, signify that the real world is black, solid, to be trusted, and worthy of being defended. In fact, the only two characters who have never been exploited by the machines are Tank and Dozer, two black men who are "100 percent pure homegrown human" since they were born in Zion, the last outpost of human civilization. The traditional colonial mission of "civilizing" the disorder and disarray of savages has been retrofitted and revamped to fit this movie's multicultural politics: the "great white hope" of the last humans on earth are black men and women, at least until this point in the film.

The position of black women in the film is far more vexed, however. The Oracle's authority and power as a black woman and a source of knowledge are undermined by her depiction as a woman baking cookies, wearing an apron, and living in a housing project with a living room full of small children. In a film so much about visual style and beautiful futuristic couture, her dowdy appearance and position securely in the lower classes seems to signify the place of black women in the future as well as the present. While the film envisions a multicultural crew resisting the white hegemony, as embodied by the agents and their agent, Cypher, it can't yet incorporate black women into this group of "real" humans except as supporting characters. Indeed, the Oracle's function as the nurturer of "potentials," or candidates (most of whom are children) for the position of the "one," continues the familiar trope of black women as mammies or supportive and willing domestic workers. The Oracle's seeming satisfaction with her traditionally racialized role as a glorified child-care worker and giver of advice to the hero represents the limits of this multiculturalist fantasy of interhuman democracy. Perhaps women of color represent the real potentials in this film, a potential that remains untapped and unrealized in this narrative of the future.

The crew of the *Nebuchadnezzer* resembles the population of Los Angeles as it is projected to look in the near future—that is, whites are a minority. However, in the face of dire anxieties regarding the future of multicultural cities and white flight from them, the ship is depicted as an ideal community, a hopeful and determinedly unglamorous coalition of oppressed workers fighting the machine. This model of community is diverse, real, gritty, dense, warm, close, and caring. They seem happy to be eating their gruel together, and united in their purpose. (Cypher is the exception to this rule, and hence the traitor.) However, the plot kills them one by one, leaving only Morpheus, Neo, and Trinity; a trinity composed of a black man, a multiracial man, and a white woman.[13] The disturbing aspect of this resolution has to do with the eradication of community as the solution to machine-induced slavery and exploitation and its replacement by the cool imagery of Neo's sunglass-clad face in the film's closing scenes as he assumes his mantle as "the one."

This notion of there only being "one" who *counts* in struggles against white oppression reduplicates the rhetoric of heroic individuality that has haunted civil rights movements since the martyrdoms of Martin Luther King Jr. and Malcolm X. Trinity and Morpheus are reduced to girlfriend and sidekick/mentor, effectively turning them into support staff for "the one." Morpheus in particular is shunted off to the sidelines and turned into a Tonto to Neo's Lone Ranger; he is rendered "serviceable," in Toni Morrison's use of the word to describe the function of blacks in American fiction (64). Morpheus's presence makes Neo even more "the one," even more a lone hero, since he stands for those things that Neo is not: bounded, limited, vulnerable, defeatable by whites. He and Trinity—whose only purpose in the plot at this point is to confirm Neo's status as "the one" by being in love with him (an all-too-familiar reminder of the uses to which female characters are put in Hollywood generally)—are discarded entirely in the film's final scene, which consists of a monologue that Neo delivers into a pay phone.

This film's ending is frustrating because it seems to take back the progressive images of race and multiracial communities that had been advanced from the beginning and replaces them with an anticommunitarian figure of authority and power: the lone hacker hero. Its ultimate message about multiculturalism in the future is to assert the solidity and abiding presence of race as a "real" thing, a serviceable thing, yet also to construct a hero whose race is so ambiguous as to be readable as white . . . or not. Keanu Reeves is a "stealth" minority; many viewers do not know that he is multiracial.[14] His casting reflects the notion of race as "residual self-image": Reeves is "read" in ways that reflect viewers' *own* preoccupations and notions of race more accurately than they reflect anything about the actor himself. Perhaps this makes him a perfect type of character to become a hero by dominating machines: half-machine himself, at least according to film reviewers' writings about his actorly (lack of) affect and style, his position on the boundary of white and other calls attention to the status of race as a matrix, no more "real" than viewers' perceptions of it. But as we know from observing hiring practices, mortgage terms, the prison-industrial complex, and the continuing segregation of neighborhoods, race doesn't need to be "real" to accomplish things in the world. As Morpheus says in reference to the matrix, "Your mind makes it real."

Neo's final monologue, which is directly addressed to the viewer, asks us to "imagine a world without limit or controls, borders or boundaries." One could read it as an echo of Morpheus's exhortation to Neo while training him to believe in himself enough to leap from one building to another: "Free your mind." The difference has to do with the rhetoric. Both of these commands ask their interlocutors to challenge authority, but with a crucial difference, a *racial* difference. "Free your mind" has long been a staple phrase of funk and popular music, much of which has an antiracist bent. Bootsy Collins's iteration of the phrase asks the listener to "free your mind and your ass will follow." En Vogue follows this up with another verse, "Be color-blind, don't be so shallow." Freeing your mind of racism is a task as hard as learning to fly from building to building, it would seem. Neo's challenge to imagine a world without limits echoes the infamous MCI commercial from the mid-1990s entitled "Anthem," which tells the viewer to "imagine a world without boundaries . . . Utopia? No! The Internet."

This is the rhetoric of commercial digital utopianism evident in so much of the commercial and corporate discourse about the Internet from the mid-1990s to the present moment. The appeal to a corporate/commercial discourse is opposed to the discourse of civil rights and multiculturalism. Its promise is to bridge the digital divide by setting up a hero who will "free the minds" of others.[15] This leaves out a scenario in which others might free their own minds. The multiracial and multicultural communities have been sacrificed to produce this leader, and most significantly, they have been depicted as eager to do so. Morpheus's determination to sacrifice himself for Neo (his cry to Trinity to take Neo away from the agents while he stays behind is "He's the only one who matters now!") is disturbing in that it constructs him, in all his blackness and, in the logic of the film, attendant realness, as an ancillary character, an adjunct or assistant to "the one," and what's more, he is depicted as accepting of life on these terms. He truly is a "supporting character" despite Fishburne's superior abilities as an actor at making the character of Morpheus seem "like a real person," verisimilitudinous in a way that Reeves never is.

Neo's promise to construct a world without boundaries places the responsibility for leadership in this quest upon the figure of the lone hacker.[17] This utopic vision of a world in which humans regain their control over machines glosses over disturbing questions about mastery in the digital age. To return to Lewis Carroll, and cite his sequel to *Alice in Wonderland, Through the Looking Glass,* the question that Humpty Dumpty directs to Alice in her travels through Wonderland, the virtually real, is "Who is to be master?" (238). This question is indeed the one to consider, and in the context of this film and our culture today it can be broken down as follows: Can whites continue to be "master" in the face of globalization and racial/cultural hybridity? Must whites (or institutionalized investments in white privilege) continue to structure access to information and media? Will the machines "win" by making us their agents? Does global capital make us all "agents" of the hegemony in ways that we can't resist or even see? Whose interests are being served in the world of the Internet? Must there be a master, a "one," or can the notion of heroic and lone leadership be replaced by community and consensus instead? What is the place of the real and the place of race in the world of the virtual?

While cyberspace may be touted both on and offline as a world without boundaries or limits, the real is ineluctably bounded. Just like the hovercraft *Nebuchadnezzar*, where all the real action in *The Matrix* occurs, it is a *place* rather than an unbounded space. The quest to understand this place, to recognize the raced and gendered cultures and people that occupy it and make it real, needs to be undertaken by the many, rather than the one. Beneath the great look of the film, the sleek and telegenic images of technology and machines, lies the insight that we are in much the same position of the enslaved humans trapped in their pods, dreaming that they are living lives of privilege that do not exploit others. This matrix of racism is the thing from which we must free our minds. While it is tempting to "deal for bliss," to buy into the prepackaged vision of the cybersociety as a democratic, raceless, "free" space, doing so means engaging in a deal that perpetuates the digital racial divide. Inequities in access, power, and representation are real. And the means of addressing these problems—community networking, funding for public technology education, better support for families and children—will not come from machines and networks, but rather from people who are willing to all eat the same "glop," so to speak. Only then can the promise of cyberspace and the Internet to democratize social relations move from the realm of wonderland's dreams to the lived realities of humanity in all its diversity.

< 4 >

"WHERE DO YOU WANT TO GO TODAY?": CYBERNETIC TOURISM, THE INTERNET, AND TRANSNATIONALITY

There is no race. There is no gender. There is no age.
There are no infirmities. There are only minds.
Utopia? No. The Internet.

— "Anthem," produced for MCI by Messner Vetere
Berger McNamee Schemetterer, 1997

The television commercial "Anthem" claims that on
the Internet, there are no infirmities, no gender, no age— "only
minds." This pure, democratic, cerebral form of communication is
touted as a utopia, a pure no-place where human interaction can
occur, as the voice-over says, "uninfluenced by the rest of it." Yet
can the "rest of it" be written out as easily as the word *race* is
crossed out on the chalkboard by the hand of an Indian girl in this
commercial?

It is "the rest of it," the specter of racial and ethnic difference
and its visual and textual representation in print and television advertisements that appeared in 1997 for Compaq, IBM, and Origin
that I will address in this chapter. The ads I will discuss all sell networking and communications technologies that depict racial difference, the "rest of it," as a visual marker. The spectacles of race in
these advertising images are designed to stabilize contemporary
anxieties that networking technology and access to cyberspace may
break down ethnic and racial differences. These advertisements
that promote the glories of cyberspace cast the viewer in the position of the tourist, and sketch out a future in which difference is either elided or put in its proper place.

I'd like to cite a striking example: the MCI advertisement sells not only MCI Internet services but also a particular kind of *content*: the idea that getting online and becoming part of a global network will liberate the user from the body with its inconvenient and limiting attributes such as race, gender, disability, and age. In a sense, it is positing a postcorporeal subjectivity, an afterimage of the body and of identity. Though "Anthem" illustrates this bracketing off of difference—racial, gendered, aged, and so on—particularly well, it is easy to find plenty of others from other technological discourses that reveal a similar sensibility, though perhaps not in as overt a way. This commercial is, however, unusually above board in its claims that telecommunications change the nature of identity.

The ironies in "Anthem" exist on several levels. For one, the advertisement positions MCI's commodity—"the largest Internet network in the world"—as a solution to social problems. This ad claims to produce a radical form of democracy that refers to and extends an "American" model of social equality and equal access. This patriotic anthem, however, is a paradoxical one: the visual images of diversity (old, young, black, white, deaf, etc.) are displayed and celebrated as spectacles of difference that the narrative simultaneously attempts to erase by claiming that MCI's product will reduce the different bodies that we see to "just minds."

The ad gestures toward a democracy founded upon disembodiment and uncontaminated by physical difference, but it must also showcase a dizzying parade of difference in order to make its point. Diversity is displayed as the sign of that which the product will eradicate. Its erasure and elision can only be understood in terms of its presence; like the word *race* on the chalkboard, it can only be crossed out if it is written or displayed. This ad writes race and poses it as both a beautiful spectacle and a vexing question. Its narrative describes a "postethnic America," to use David Hollinger's phrase, where these categories will be made not to count. The supposedly liberal and progressive tone of this ad camouflages its depiction of race as something to be eliminated, or made "not to count," through technology. If computers and networks can help us to communicate without "the rest of it," that residue of difference with its power to disturb, disrupt, and challenge, then we can all exist in a world "without boundaries."

A television commercial by AT&T that aired during the 1996

Olympics asks the viewer to "imagine a world without limits—AT&T believes communication can make it happen." Like "Anthem," this narrative posits a connection between networking and a democratic ethos in which differences will be elided. In addition, it resorts to a similar visual strategy—it depicts a black man in track shorts leaping over the Grand Canyon.

Like many of the ads by high-tech and communications companies that aired during the Olympics, this one has an "international" or multicultural flavor that seemed to celebrate national and ethnic identities. This world without limits is represented by vivid and often sublime images of displayed ethnic and racial difference in order to bracket them off as exotic and irremediably "other." Images of this other as primitive, anachronistic, and picturesque decorate the landscape of these ads.

Microsoft's recent television and print media campaign markets access to personal computing and Internet connectivity by describing these activities as a form of travel. Travel and tourism, like networking technology, are commodities which define the privileged industrialized "first world" subject, and they situate him in the position of the one who looks, the one who has access, the one who communicates. Microsoft's omnipresent slogan "Where do you want to go today?" rhetorically places this consumer in the position of the user with unlimited choice; access to Microsoft's technology and networks promises the consumer a "world without limits" where he can possess an idealized mobility. Microsoft's promise to transport the user to new (cyber)spaces where desire can be fulfilled is enticing in its very vagueness, offering a seemingly open-ended invitation to travel and new experiences. A sort of technologically enabled transnationality is evoked here, but it is one that directly addresses the "first world" user, whose position on the network will allow him to metaphorically go wherever he likes.

This dream or fantasy of ideal travel common to networking advertisements constructs a destination that can look like an African safari, a trip to the Amazonian rain forest, or a camel caravan in the Egyptian desert. The iconography of the travelogue or tourist attraction in these ads places the viewer in the position of the tourist who, in Dean MacCannell's words, "simply collects experiences of difference (different people, different places)" and "emerges as a miniature clone of the old Western philosophical subject, thinking itself unified, central, in control, etc., mastering Otherness and profiting from it" (xv). Networking ads that promise the viewer control and mastery over technology and communications discursively and visually link this power to a vision of the other which, in contrast to the mobile and networked tourist/user, isn't going anywhere. The continued presence of stable signifiers of otherness in telecommunications advertising guarantees the Western subject that his position, wherever he may choose to go today, remains privileged.

An ad from Compaq (see fig. 4.1) that appeared in the *Chronicle of Higher Education* reads, "Introducing a world where the words 'you can't get there from here' are never heard." It depicts a sandstone mesa with the inset image of a monitor from which two schoolchildren gaze curiously at the sight. The ad is selling "Compaq networked multimedia. With it, the classroom is no longer a destination, it's a starting point." Like the Microsoft and AT&T slogans, this one links networks with privileged forms of travel, and reinforces the metaphor by visually depicting sights that viewers associate with tourism. The networked classroom is envisioned as a glass window from which users can consume the sights of travel as if they were tourists.

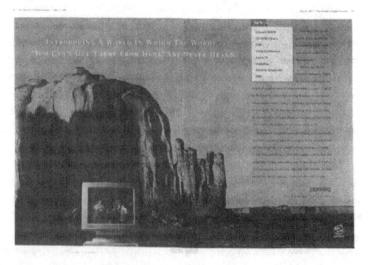

FIGURE 4.1. Mesa (Compaq)

FIGURE 4.2. Rain forest (Compaq)

Another ad from the Compaq series shows the same children admiring the rain forest from their places inside the networked classroom, signified by the frame of the monitor (see fig. 4.2). The tiny box on the upper righthand side of the image evokes the distinctive menu bar of a Windows product, and frames the whole ad for its viewer as a window onto an "other" world.

The sublime beauty of the mesa and the lush pastoral images of the rain forest are nostalgically quoted here in order to assuage an anxiety about the environmental effects of cybertechnology. In a world where sandstone mesas and rain forests are becoming increasingly rare, partly as a result of industrialization, these ads position networking as a benign, "green" type of product that will preserve the beauty of nature, at least as an image on the screen. As John Macgregor Wise puts it, this is part of the modernist discourse that envisioned electricity as "transcendent, pure and clean," unlike mechanical technology (n.p.). The same structures of metaphor that allow this ad to dub the experience of using networked communications "travel" also enables it to equate an image of a rain forest with Nature—with a capital N. The enraptured American schoolchildren, with their backpacks and French braids, are framed as user-travelers. With the assistance of Compaq, they have found their way to a world that seems to be without limits, one in which the images of Nature are as good as or better than the reality.

The virtually real rain forest and mesa participate in a postcyberspace paradox of representation—the locution *virtual reality* suggests that the line or limit between the authentic sight/site and its simulation has become blurred. This discourse has become familiar, and was anticipated by Jean Baudrillard before the advent of the Internet. Familiar as it is, the Internet and its representations in media such as advertising have refigured the discourse in different contours. The ads that I discuss attempt to stabilize the slippery relationship between the virtual and the real by insisting upon the monolithic visual differences between "first" and "third world" landscapes and people.

This virtual field trip frames nature as a tourist sight and figures Compaq as the educational tour guide. In this post-Internet culture of simulation in which we live, it is increasingly necessary for stable, iconic images of nature and the other to be evoked in the world of technology advertising. These images guarantee and gesture toward the unthreatened and unproblematic existence of a destination for travel, a place whose natural beauties and exotic natives will somehow remain intact and attractive. If technology will indeed make everyone, everything, and every place the same, as "Anthem" claims in its ambivalent way, then where is there left to go? What is there left to see? What is the use of being asked where you want to go today if every place is just like here? Difference, in the form of exotic places or exotic people, must be demonstrated iconographically in order to shore up the Western user's identity as herself. As Caren Kaplan writes, "[C]reated out of increasing leisure time in industrialized nations and driven by a need to ascertain identity and location in a world that undermines the certainty of those categories, the tourist acts as an agent of modernity" (58). The tourist's need to reorient herself is made all the more pressing by the radically destabilizing effects of cyberspace, which blows older notions of "identity" and "location" out of the water. And as Caplan goes on to note, the links among modernity, travel, and colonialism are strong and of long standing.[1] The idyllic image of an Arab on his camel, with the pyramids picturesquely squatting in the background, belongs in a coffee table book (see fig. 4.3). The timeless quality of this image of an exotic other untouched by modernity is disrupted by the cartoon dialogue text, which reads, "What do you say we head back and download the results of the equestrian finals?" This dissonant use of contemporary, vernacular, American technoslang is supposed to be read comically; the man is meant to look unlike anyone who would speak these words.

This gap between the exotic otherness of the image and the familiarity of the American rhetoric can be read as more than an attempt at humor, however. IBM, whose slogan "Solution for a small planet" is contained in an icon button in the lower left-hand side of the image, is literally putting these incongruous words into the other's mouth, thus demonstrating the hegemonic power of its "high speed information network" to make the planet smaller by causing everyone to speak the *same* language—computerspeak. The Arab man's position as the exotic other must be emphasized and foregrounded in order for this strategy to work, for the image's

FIGURE 4.3. Arab and camel (IBM)

appeal rests upon its evocation of the exotic. The rider's classical antique "look and feel" atop his Old Testament camel guarantee that his access to a high-speed network will not rob us, the tourists/viewers, of the spectacle of his difference. In the phantasmatic world of Internet advertising, he can download all the results he likes, so long as his visual appeal to us as viewers reassures us that we are still in the position of the tourist, the Western subject, whose privilege it is to enjoy him in all his anachronistic glory.

These ads claim a world without boundaries for us, the consumers and target audience, and by so doing they show us exactly where and what these boundaries are, and that is ethnic and racial. Rather than being effaced, these dividing lines are evoked repeatedly. In addition, the ads sanitize and idealize their depictions of the other and otherness by deleting all references that might threaten their status as timeless icons. In the camel image, the sky is an untroubled blue, the pyramids have fresh, clean, sharp outlines, and there are no signs whatsoever of pollution, roadkill, litter, or airborne warning and control systems.

Including these "real life" images in the advertisement would disrupt the picture it presents us of an other whose "unspoiled" qualities are so highly valued by tourists. Indeed, as Trinh Minh-ha notes, even very sophisticated tourists are quick to reject experiences that challenge their received notions of authentic otherness. Minh-ha writes, "The Third World representative the modern sophisticated public ideally seeks is the *unspoiled* African, Asian, or Native American, who remains more preoccupied with his/her image as the *real* native—the *truly different*—than with the issues of hegemony, feminism, and social change" (88). Great pains are taken in this ad to make the camel rider appear real, truly different from us, and "authentic" in order to build an idealized other whose unspoiled nature shores up the tourist's sense that he is indeed seeing the "real" thing. In the post-Internet world of simulation, "real" things are fixed and preserved in images such as these in order to anchor the Western viewing subject's sense of himself as a privileged and mobile viewer.

Since the conflicts of Mogadishu, Sarajevo, and Zaire (all images contained elsewhere in the magazines from which these ads came), ethnic difference in the world of Internet advertising is visually "cleansed" of its divisive, problematic, tragic connotations. The ads function as corrective texts for readers deluged with images of racial conflicts and bloodshed both at home and abroad. These advertisements put the world right; their claims for better living (and better boundaries) through technology are graphically acted out in idealized images of others who miraculously speak like "us" but still look like "them."

The Indian man pictured in an IBM print advertisment that appeared in January 1996, whose iconic Indian elephant gazes sidelong at the viewer as he affectionately curls his trunk around his owner's neck, has much in common with his Egyptian counterpart in the previous ad. (The ad's text tells us that his name is Sikander, making him somewhat less generic than his counterpart, but not much. Where is the last name?) The thematics of this series produced for IBM play upon the depiction of ethnic, racial, and linguistic differences, usually all at the same time, in order to highlight the hegemonic power of IBM's technology. IBM's television ads (there were several produced and aired in this same series in 1997) were memorable because they were all subtitled vignettes with Italian nuns, Japanese surgeons, and Norwegian skiers engaged in their quaint and distinctively ethnic pursuits, but united in their use of IBM networking machines. The sounds of foreign languages being spoken in television ads had their own ability to shock and attract attention, all to the same end—the one thing that was spoken in English, albeit heavily accented English, was "IBM."

Thus, the transnational language, the one designed to end all barriers between speakers, the speech that everyone can pronounce and that cannot be translated or incorporated into another tongue, turns out not to be Esperanto, but rather IBM-speak, the language of American corporate technology. The foreignness of the other is exploited here to remind the viewer who may fear that IBM-speak will make the world smaller in undesirable ways (for example, that they might compete for our jobs, move into our neighborhoods, go to our schools) that the other is still picturesque. This classically orientalized other, such as the camel rider and Sikander, is marked as sufficiently different from us, the projected viewers, in order to encourage us to retain our positions as privileged tourists and users.

Sikander's cartoon bubble, emblazoned across his face and his elephant's, asks, "How come I keep trashing my hardware every 9 months?!" This sentence can be read as a rhetorical example of what postcolonial theorist and novelist Salman Rushdie has termed "globalizing Coca-Colonization." Again, the language of technology, with its hacker-dude vernacular, is figured here as the transnational tongue, miraculously emerging from every mouth. Possible fears that the exoticness and heterogeneity of the other will be siphoned off or eradicated by his use of homogeneous technospeak are eased by the visual impact of the elephant, whose trunk frames Sikander's face.

Elephants, rain forests, and unspoiled mesas are all endangered markers of cultural difference that represent specific stereotyped ways of being other to Western eyes. If we did not know that Sikander was a "real" Indian (as opposed to an Indo-American, Indo-Canadian, or Indo-Anglian) the presence of his elephant as well as the text's reference to Nirvana, proves to us that he is through the power of familiar images. We are meant to assume that even after Sikander's hardware problems are solved by IBM's consultants, "who consider where you are as well are where you're headed," he will still look as picturesque, as "Indian" as he did pre-IBM.

Two other ads, part of the same series produced by IBM, feature more ambiguously ethnic figures. The first of these depicts a Latina girl who is asking her teacher, Mrs. Alvarez, how to "telnet" to a remote server. She wears a straw hat, which makes reference to the American Southwest. Though she is only eight or ten years old, her speech has already acquired the distinctive sounds of technospeak—for example, she uses *telnet* as a verb. The man in the second advertisement, an antique-looking fellow with old-fashioned glasses, a dark tunic, dark skin, and an untidy beard proclaims that "you're hosed when a virus sneaks into your hard drive." He, too, speaks the transnational vernacular—the diction of Wayne and Garth from *Wayne's World* has "sneaked into *his* hard drive" like a rhetorical virus. These images, like the preceding ones, enact a sort of cultural ventriloquism that demonstrates the hegemonic power of American technospeak. The identifiably ethnic faces that utter these words, with their distinctive props and costumes attest, however, to the importance of this otherness as a marker of a difference the ads strive to preserve.

Wired magazine, like *Time, Smithsonian,* the *New Yorker,* and

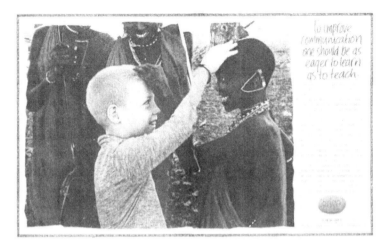

FIGURE 4.4. Black boy and white boy (Origin)

the *Chronicle of Higher Education* directs its advertising chiefly toward upper-middle-class white readers. In addition, it is read mainly by men, has an unabashedly libertarian bias, and its stance toward technology is generally utopian. Unlike the other ads discussed here, the one for Origin that appeared in *Wired* directly and overtly poses ethnicity and cultural difference as part of a political and commercial dilemma that its product, Origin networks, can solve (see fig. 4.4). The text reads,

> We believe that wiring machines is the job, but connecting people the art. Which means besides skills you also need wisdom and understanding. An understanding of how people think and communicate. And the wisdom to respect the knowledge and cultures of others. Because only then can you create systems and standards they can work with. And common goals which all involved are willing to achieve.

The image of an African boy, surrounded by his tribe, performing the *Star Trek* "Vulcan mind-meld" gesture with a redhaired and extremely pale boy, centrally situates the white child, whose arm is visible in an unbroken line, as the figure who is supposedly as willing to learn as he is to teach.

The text implies, however, that the purpose of the white boy's encounter with an African boy and his tribe is for him to learn just enough about them to create the "systems and standards that THEY can work with." The producer of marketable knowledge, the setter of networking and software-language standards, is still defined here as the Western subject. This image, which could have come out of *National Geographic* any time in the last hundred years, participates in the familiar iconography of colonialism and its contemporary cousin, tourism. And in keeping with this association, it depicts the African as unspoiled and authentic. Its appeal to travel across national and geographical borders as a means of understanding the other, "the art of connecting people," is defined as a commodity that this ad and others produced by networking companies sell *along with* their fiber optics and consulting services.

The notion of the computer-enabled "global village" envisioned by Marshall McLuhan (93) also participates in this rhetoric which links exotic travel and tourism with technology. The Origin image comments on the nature of the global village by making it quite clear to the viewer that despite technology's claims to radically and instantly level cultural and racial differences (or in a more extreme statement, such as that made by MCI's "Anthem," to literally cross them out) there will always be villages full of "real" Africans, looking just as they always have.

It is part of the business of advertising to depict utopias: ideal depictions of being that correctively reenvision the world and prescribe a solution to its ills in the form of a commodity of some sort. And like tourist pamphlets, they often propose that their products will produce, in Dean MacCannell's phrase, a "utopia of difference," such as has been pictured in many Benetton and Coca-Cola advertising campaigns.

Coca-Cola's slogan from the seventies and eighties, "I'd like to teach the world to sing," both predates and prefigures these ads by IBM, Compaq, Origin, and MCI. The ads picture people who are black, white, young, old, and so on holding hands and forming a veritable Rainbow Coalition of human diversity. These singers are united by their shared song and—more importantly—their consumption of Coke. The viewer, who it was hoped would infer that the beverage was the direct cause of these diverse people overcoming their ethnic and racial differences, was given the same message that many Internet-related advertisements give us today. The message is that cybertechnology, like Coke, will magically strip users down to "just minds," all singing the same corporate anthem.

And what of the "rest of it," the raced and ethnic body that cyberspace's "Anthem" claims to leave behind? It seems that the fantasy terrain of advertising is loath to leave out this marked body because it represents the exotic other that both attracts us with its beauty and picturesqueness and reassures us of our own identities as *not other*. The "rest of it" is visually quoted in these images and then pointedly marginalized and established *as other*. The iconography of these advertising images demonstrates that the corporate image factory *needs* images of the other in order to depict its product: a technological utopia of difference. It is not, however, a utopia *for* the other or one that includes it in any meaningful or progressive way. Rather, it proposes an ideal world of virtual social and cultural reality based on specific methods of "othering," a project that I would call the globalizing Coca-Colonization of cyberspace and the media complex within which it is embedded.

< 5 >

MENU-DRIVEN IDENTITIES:
MAKING RACE HAPPEN ONLINE

What happens to race on the World Wide Web? And why should we assume that *anything at all* happens to race on the web? Many proponents of cyberutopia claim that the Internet is inherently democratic and color-blind because its users can engage with it anonymously. Because their race and/or gender need be known to others when they engage in web chat, post texts to websites or news groups, or send e-mail, some believe that users' identities can be "freed" from race when on the web.

Users can express their subjectivity while mouse clicking their way through the web; they create their individual paths through the endless series of menus and hierarchical lists. The vastness of the web has contributed to the popularity of "portals" to the Internet such as Excite, Yahoo! and Lycos that mediate the users' experience by offering search engine assistance, news and weather reports, searchable databases, advertising, and, most importantly, a friendly and familiar "front end" to cyberspace. However, web interface design, such as that evident in web portals, reveals assumptions about users' race and ethnicity. Though the web is a relatively new medium, it has been around enough for its interface to have become naturalized. That is to say, users and critics alike may tend to focus primarily on its content and neglect the political aspects of its design, or even fail to recognize interface design decisions *as* political.

Rather surprisingly, even websites that focus on ethnic and racial identity and community often possess interface design features that force reductive, often archaic means of defining race upon the user. This produces a new kind of cybertyping, one that encompasses the user's racial identity within the paradigm of the "clickable box"—one box among many on the menu of identity choices. When users are given no choice other than to select the "race" or "ethnicity" to which they belong, and are given no means to define or modify the terms or categories available to them, then identities that do not appear on the menu are essentially foreclosed on and erased. This limits the ways that race can happen in cyberspace and also denies the possibility of a *mestiza* consciousness on these sites.[1] This has important theoretical repercussions as well as practical ones, for the category of *mestiza* has functioned as an ideological football, at least among theorists of cybercultures, for reasons I will discuss in further detail later.

Ethnic identity websites may or may not be progressive. If we look beyond the web for ways that the Internet can be used to promote a sense of racial and ethnic community and identity, we can see alternative uses of the net. These uses propagate a sense of racial identity that spreads via rhizomatic networks of e-mail recipients and forwarders.[2] These webs of affinity don't always happen on the web,[3] and though these e-mail–based webs may display some forms of racial stereotyping, they don't cybertype racial identity in the same way that some commercial web interfaces do. They manage to perform an end run around menu-driven identities, and their robust, guerrilla-like means of transmission serve as an apt example of a "lower," more accessible kind of technology in cyberspace in contrast to the high-tech cyberspace extolled by corporations. These rhizomes encourage racial and ethnic border crossing and a hybrid, flexible, constructed sense of race that at least partially fulfills the Internet's promise to make race matter online in ways that are not commodified, rigid, or racist.

Users are often overwhelmed by the sheer mass of data on the web. The anxiety caused by this carnivalesque riot of texts and images mirrors the unease that readers of postmodern fictions experience. The web is much more pleasurable to use if one has a sense of control and order over the material; hence the popularity of portals and their integrated search engines. The pleasure of unbounded texts like the web is an acquired taste. Just as the reader new to postmodern fiction needs tools such as literary analysis in order to appreciate the quality of this experience, so, too, do users seek out "guided readings" of the web. Corporate portals are all too happy to perform this service in exchange for the chance to expose the viewer to carefully targeted online advertising. The market for services that shape the user's experience is large and lucrative. As the phenomenal success of companies such as Yahoo! and Excite in the mid- to late 1990s has shown, web portals are big business. As the web grows larger, forms of organization and mediation between its content and the user become increasingly necessary.

As the bonds between commerce and information grow stronger, it is important to ask, What structures of organization are mediating users' experience with the web, and how do these structures contribute to the ways race is expressed and experienced online? A close look at portals reveals that they are often structured in ways that reaffirm stereotyped racial categories rather than challenge them. Portals condition a particular way of reading the web that doesn't actually change its content, but creates a particular kind of reading that is mediated by an interface, and thus a particular type of reader.

Portals impose order upon the web's enormous collection of data by presenting the user with a series of choices. In the case of Excite's list of websites about "cultures and groups," the user is asked to make choices about racial identity as well. When I entered the search term *race* into Excite's search engine, I received a number of results that were clearly about boat racing and horse racing. This type of category slippage is an everyday occurrence on the web. I then entered the term *racial* and was directed to a page that contained a list of clickable categories that I was encouraged to "try first." This list of ten categories reads as follows:

African Diaspora
Asian-American
Gay and Lesbian
Community Services
Latino Culture
Men's Issues
Native American Culture
Religion
Virtual Worlds
Women's Issues[4]

I chose "Asian American," and was presented with a series of increasingly specific categories, such as Japanese, Chinese, and Korean. I noticed a few things; the arrangement of this menu only allowed me to click upon one category at a time. (The incorporation of frames into Netscape's 1997 release of its web browser Navigator permits the user to keep several windows open simultaneously; nonetheless, even while using multiple frames I can only pursue one path of webbed reading at a time.) While my identity might encompass women's issues *and* Asian American *and* Native American *and* gay and lesbian issuess, all at the same time and in more or less equal measure depending on what I am doing or how I conceive of myself at the time, the list reifies these identities and sets them up as discrete and separate from each other. In other words, it forces the user to choose "what" they are, and allows only one choice at a time. This interface feature enforces a menu-driven sense of personal identity that works by progressively narrowing the choices of subject positions available to the user, an outcome that seems to fly in the face of claims that the Internet allows for a more fluid, free, unbounded sense of identity than had been available in other media—or, indeed, in the world—before.

Far from encouraging the user's sense of a "multiple self" enabled by this technology that Sherry Turkle celebrates in her writings, the structure of this menu works to close off the possibility of alternate or hybrid definitions of racial identity. If I attempt to read recursively by clicking on the "back" button I can attempt to bring all of these categories together, but the unavoidable necessity of choosing one first still remains. Excite's structure of ranked menus and links, which seems on the face of it to be all about choice, in fact offers no other choice.

While the category *African Diaspora* does seem more nuanced and historically grounded than the terms *black*, or *African American*, the latter of which would exclude non-Americans of African descent, this hypertextual list of identity choices reminds me of nothing other than the dreaded U.S. Census form, which has only now made the category "Other" available to describe racial identity. This category has become necessary in an increasingly multicultural and multiethnic America where old categories for describing identity are at best misleading and at worst inaccurate, and its existence indicates a new, more complex understanding of race. However, Excite's list reinforces old notions of racial identity as linked to black-and-white definitions because it offers such a limited range of choices, none of which may reflect the identity of the actual user who is using the web to find information about her race in particular or race in general. While this menu isn't requiring the user to identify her race by clicking on a link, the experience of seeing this list transferred from the outmoded and at times overtly racist language of demographic census taking and identity taxonomies to the web brings to the fore the issue of ethnicity and race as categories ranked with—yet distinct from—others. Excite's list literally highlights these categories in differently colored fonts that visually signify their function as branches on the "decision tree" of racial identity.

Excite's guided reading of race on the web performs another interesting textual move: it lumps gender, sexual orientation, religion, and age together with race. This organizing of identity does not include "white" as a category; it is not on the menu at all. This omission is a disturbing example of the colonialist or imperialist gaze that sets up a racial other; whiteness is defined by its invisibility rather than its presence. The racial category of "whiteness" is assumed to be a default option, thus creating a guided reading of the web that assumes that its reader *is* white. This structure does equal disservice to whites, who are implicitly assumed not to possess a racial identity at all since it is omitted from the list, and nonwhites, whose experiences as users are excluded.

Since "men's issues" are included in the list, as are "women's issues," it seems that gender is one of the forks in the path of reading identity on the web. The decision to include this category acknowledges the existence of a male identity while excluding the possibility of a distinctively white one.

There is very little published on the topic of hypertext, interface design, and race. While many scholars have indicated a need for further research, few have engaged with the rigorous affinities between the web as a cultural and discursive practice, a "made" space, and the field of signifying practices that we call "race." Mark Poster's work is a notable exception: though he does not address the web specifically, in *The Second Media Age* the chapter entitled "Multiculturalism and the Postmodern Media Age" he points out that "as the second media age unfolds and permeates everyday practice, one political issue will be the construction of new combinations of technology with multiple genders and ethnicities" (42). Certainly, since 1995, the year in which Poster wrote these words, the web has become a prime harbinger of the second media age in the sense that it "permeates everyday practice," at least for white middle-class Americans. His work also calls attention to the crucial element of the politics of authorship in cybernetic spaces; the landscape architects of the web's forking-path structures such as portals are largely white male software engineers. Portals are highly commodified products of Silicon Valley big business; they are produced via multiple partnerships with enormously profitable multinational companies such as IBM, Microsoft, and Compaq, and as such are hardly the spaces that would prioritize the articulation of minority identities. Just as we cannot expect that popular market-driven media such as film, advertising, and television will necessarily make it a part of their mission to represent race in progressive ways (or indeed at all), we should not assume that web portals will. Far from attributing the responsibility for this state of affairs to any specific individual designer or corporation, envisioning the web as one form of popular media among others allows an analysis of our culture's limited ways of looking at race.

Like their namesake, those tiny windows in submarines, portals offer an extremely limited and constricted view of the world. The successive series of lists they offer omit many identity choices—among them "interracial" and "white/European."

This is particularly disappointing when we take into account the predictions from only a few years ago that the Internet would serve to level out racial inequality; initially, hopes were high regarding its potential. Susan Zickmund writes, in "Approaching the Radical Other: The Discursive Culture of Cyberspace," that the openness of the Internet "may [. . .] endanger the notion of a closed community" and "could become an ally in the struggle against bigotry and racism" (252). This optimism is echoed in Turkle's assertion that the "more fluid sense of self" engendered by the Internet "allows a greater capacity for acknowledging diversity. It makes it easier to accept the array of our and other's inconsistent personae—perhaps with humor, perhaps with irony. We do not feel compelled to rank

or judge the elements of our multiplicity. We do not feel to compelled to exclude what does not fit" (262).

Libertarian rhetoric, such as that often seen in *Wired* magazine's
editorials, is apt to display a more radical optimism; its maxim that
"information wants to be free" assumes that freeing information by
making it available on the Net will liberate users from their bodies
and hence from inconvenient side effects such as racism and sexism. The equation seems simple: If no one's body is visible while
participating in cyberspace, theoretically racism and bigotry cannot
exist at that time and in that place. This notion of the web as a cure
for racism is attractive, and indeed, such web features as chat
rooms have enabled unique kinds of racial discourse and social interaction to occur that were impossible before (such as cross-racial
role playing).

Unfortunately, the web has failed to live up to these predictions,
as I point out in chapter 2. Far from becoming sensitized to what it
feels like to be another race in cyberspace, many users masquerading as racial minorities in chat spaces tend to depict themselves in
ways that simply repeat and reenact old racial stereotypes. It is not
uncommon in many multiple-user domains and role-playing cyberspaces to come across users masquerading as samurai and geishas,
complete with swords, kimonos, and other paraphernalia lifted
from older media such as film and television. This is hardly a version of ethnicity that contemporary Asian or Asian-American users
can identify with, especially considering that neither samurai nor
geisha really exist anymore. More to the point, this type of play
reenacts an anachronistic version of "Asianness" that reveals more
about users' fantasies and desires than it does about what it "feels
like" to be Asian either on- or offline.

Conversations about how the web can "wipe out" race may obscure the fact that users do indeed possess bodies that are raced—
bodies that are denied housing and discriminated against in job
interviews and that suffer institutional forms of racism offline. Despite the various techniques the web offers for hiding one's race, the
fact that race deeply impacts most users' experiences in the world
cannot be erased. This leads to another crucial aspect of race and
the web: demographics and racial representation. Borrowing a notion from President Bill Clinton, does the web "look like America?

Should it, and does that matter? If so, why, and in what way should the web look like America?

Web demographics are always in flux. It has been known for some time, however, that racial minorities use the web less than do whites. Donna Hoffman and Thomas Novak's "Bridging the Digital Divide: The Impact of Race on Computer Access and Internet Use" states that "whites are more likely than African Americans to have access to a computer at home and work, while African Americans are more likely to *want* access." Racial minorities have less access to the web than do their white counterparts; they are underrepresented, partly because of the cost—both financial and cultural—of acquiring Net literacy. This underrepresentation of nonwhites online has its roots in historical developments in American educational policy, as Jonathan Sterne describes in his essay "The Computer Race Meets Computer Classes: How Computers in Schools Helped Shape the Racial Topography of the Internet." Governmental funding to support computer instruction in public schools in the 1980s tended to favor upper-middle-class and white students who were, ironically, already those most likely to possess access to computers in the home. Policies such as these, which provided white students with a head start with regard to this technology, have perpetuated the vicious cycle of minority lack of access to computing in general, and the Internet in particular, that is still playing itself out today.

Hoffman and Novak's "Bridging the Digital Divide" was a major force in bringing issues of race and cyberspace to the forefront of public debate. Since its publication, a series that follows up its implications, entitled "Falling through the Net: Toward Digital Inclusion," was released in 1999 by the U.S. government, and partnerships have been formed to "bridge the digital divide." This study proved so influential that the term *digital divide* has become a catchphrase of sorts and is now commonly invoked in both mainstream and alternative media. However, one factor neglected in these studies is the distinction between the user and the producer of Internet content. Hoffman and Novak's study examines the incidence of African American *usage* of the Internet and the web; a separate yet equally important issue in regard to race and the web is that of *authorship*: What are the racial demographics of those who write the content, design the interfaces, and create the search engines that make up the web and condition our readings of it? If African Americans are underrepresented as web users, they are even more underrepresented as web builders.[5]

This has serious implications for "digital culture" generally. (I put this term in quotes partly to acknowledge its overuse as a cliché, but also to point out its status as a misnomer; while we tend to think of culture as rich, varied, layered, anchored in a specific locality, and possessing depth, digital culture as envisioned by popular media and as represented by corporate portals is strikingly consistent as to look and feel. In other words, the visual style of portals tends to be flat, generic, and undiverse—including that of the "ethnic identity" portals such as AsianAvenue.com and Black-Planet.com. Indeed, digital culture as it exists today is a monoculture, for reasons that have already been discussed. It is most decidedly not "multicultural.") The web is increasingly becoming a widespread and at times unavoidable aspect of modern culture. Access to jobs, networking, and professional advancement, especially in lucrative high-tech fields, quite often *require* web use. The continued exclusion or underrepresentation of minorities as web builders may mean that interfaces continue to offer the same limited range of choices that are tailored, however unconsciously, to white users. Indeed, it is the very unconsciousness of this process that makes the process itself difficult to combat or even identify. (Young, highly educated workers at web-design companies in urban areas are in fact quite likely to possess sincere "liberal" views vis-à-vis race.)

It is thus vital that we acquire and use theoretical tools for analyzing interface design and its unspoken biases. It is all the more important that we do this when we take into account the popularity and increasing hegemony of the web; its dominance gives it the potential to have an immense impact on reforming our notions of race if we can successfully increase minority participation in its design and take minorities as users into account.

The web is the most popular incarnation of the Internet, and at the time of this writing comes the closest (albeit not very close at all) to constituting a "public sphere," a virtual agora where users can meet and exchange the kind of discourse that builds community.

The web's accessibility and its potential to focus on communities and community building offers unprecedentedly rich opportunities for a discussion of how identities, racial and otherwise, are being constructed and deployed. The web is not yet, however, a public sphere in a truly democratic and racially inclusive sense: demographic studies have shown that while gender and racial diversity on the web and the Internet in general is improving, this is primarily because the web started out as—and is still primarily—a domain of the white upper-middle-class male user. Thus, these statistics can be misleading; since there were initially such small numbers of minority users, any increase at all can seem significant.

Yet just as this medium may result in interactions that reenact and recapitulate racist discourse and behavior, so too can the web function to reinforce a "ranking and judging" of "multiplicity." The multiple interlacing discourses of racial identity can—as in the case of Excite's page, which offers to "track down" your race and ethnicity if you plug your last name into its search field—as easily serve to reinforce biological and essential notions of race as they can deconstruct and challenge them.

The web has come to stand for the Internet in the minds of most users; practically speaking, the web *is* cyberspace. This was emphatically not the case as recently as 1995; prior to that date, users had to master the use of several different clients, or separate programs, to read e-mail, to chat with other users, to download files, to view graphic images, or to decode sound files. The web is the most elastic and hardy of electronic media forms: heteroglossic, multigeneric, channeled, integrated, and polymorphous, like the novel as characterized by Mikhail Bakhtin it has successfully assimilated and incorporated other cybergenres such as chat, Java applets, e-mail, and so on, and is successfully subsuming them into itself. As web browser applications have become more fully featured, users now need never leave the web in order to write and read e-mail, download files, listen to music, and chat.

In addition, the web has the aura of truth. I often describe it to others as a garage sale of information: while you will always find *something*, the value, accuracy, and relevance of what you find can be doubtful. For scholars and students, especially, the web requires that they use their critical agency more carefully than they might while scanning the *Encyclopaedia Britannica*. This caution needs to be kept in mind at all times, since the web's information comes to us in slick, telegenic, attractive images and text that give the impression of authenticity and legitimacy and can therefore seem true. All of this data comes to us on the same desktop—out of the same pipe, so to speak—and thus represents actual scholarship and other assorted data ranging from (at best) misinformation to (at worst) crackpot theories as all somehow equal to each other.

These misleading sites of information, which often come delivered in the glossy, deceiving guise of a "legitimate" home page, can also contain hate speech. It's easy to illustrate this phenomenon through numerous examples: when I recently plugged the search term *Holocaust* into a popular search engine, I was directed to a neo-Nazi website that made the case that the Holocaust never happened, as well as to sites such as the "American Holocaust Memorial—memorial to the holocaust of abortion and its correlations with the Nazi holocaust."

As this particular example shows, the web is indeed a place where race "happens," even when you aren't looking for it, and is constructed not only through the content of the texts on the Internet but also by particular forms of electronic linkage, ranked menus, search engines, and other forms of mediation that guide our readings of them. In this example—of the linkage of the Holocaust to anti-choice militant groups enabled by hypertext—race happens *with* gender, in ways visible and striking that they could not occur in other media. What's more, race happens on the web in ways unique to the medium of hypertext and web menus. The web has the ability to challenge notions of canonized racial and "other" histories and identities, yet can also force particular racialized identity choices on the part of the user.

Feminist critic Gloria Anzaldúa is not generally cited as a source in essays on technology, perhaps because her work tends not to address such issues head on. On the other hand, Anzaldúa's critical vocabulary—her take on multiculturalism and the cultural means by which fragmentary *mestiza* or racially and culturally mixed selves are articulated, marginalized, and created—proves extremely useful in describing the ways that recursive, resistant readings of "portaled" hypertexts can be imagined. Anzaldúa provides a model of resistant reading that challenges menu-driven racialism, and most importantly demonstrates the ways that reading and writing, on the web or otherwise, can become revolutionary acts.

In *Borderlands/La Frontera*, Anzaldúa has written her own search engine for racial and gender identity. She continually invokes and clicks through search terms such as *white, colored, queer,* and *race*, and has created her own kind of multicultural text that allows these terms to exist in webbed relation to each other, and to come together in the figure of the new mestiza. The mestiza has a "webbed" consciousness; her mission is to "take inventory [. . .]. Just what did she inherit from her ancestors? This weight on her back—which is the baggage from the Indian mother, which the baggage from the Spanish father, which the baggage from the Anglo?" (82).

As the mestiza clicks her way through the various and divergent paths of identity one could envision her working through the Excite list and clicking *every* keyword and search path. The mestiza on the web, as anywhere, "reinterprets history and, using new symbols, she shapes new myths. She adopts new perspectives towards the darkskinned, women, and queers. She strengthens her tolerance (and intolerance) for ambiguity" (82).

Indeed, web portals function in a similarly double way; they encourage tolerance by acknowledging "diverse" identities, yet create ambiguities about identities that fall between the cracks of hierarchical lists, those sites or "no-places" of hybrid being that seem to hover phantasmatically between the fine strands of the portaled web. What if you just don't fit into any of the categories available on the list, or do not consider any one of them *dominant* but are nonetheless required by the interface to choose one first?

Anzaldúa's manifesto, "La Consciencia de la Mestiza: Towards a New Consciousness," was written in 1987 and thus predates the web by several years; it nonetheless functions as a portal, one that debunks the notion that one must necessarily choose a single racial, gender, or ethnic identity. It seeks to permit an infinitely "clickable" interface to culture: the mestiza, "like others having or living in more than one culture," gets "multiple, often opposing messages. The coming together of two self-consistent but habitually incompatible frames of reference causes *un choque*, a cultural collision" (78). This "shock" has a political valence, as does the experience of web users whose encounters with portals of ethnicity force them to take paths that lead to stereotyped and limited destinations. Like the web itself, Anzaldúa's text fails to come to solid conclusions about these terms; the search remains open ended. Her guided reading is like an ideal notion of hypertext: it is an interface in which taxonomic lists and nested menus of terms blur and converge. And like the web, hers is a diverse and multigeneric text incorporating poetry, different languages, varied forms of address, and revisionist history.

As portals come to overlay the web and become hegemonic and dominant means for navigating it, it is all the more important that we become sensitive to the ways that these mediations categorize racial and gender identity.

When the new mestiza on the web grasps her mouse and starts clicking she reads in a participatory way rather than a passive one. She surfs through cyberspace, never settling with just *one* category on the list, always moving on to the next and the next. She builds webs between categories and performs the vital work of resistant reading. However, as portals become Disneyfied corporate interfaces and flashy, franchised front ends to cyberspace,⁰ this work becomes increasingly difficult, requiring immense efforts to work and read against the grain.

As I mentioned earlier, Anzaldúa is generally not cited as a reference regarding technology, but she has been adopted by at least one well-known critic of cybercultures, Allucquère Rosanne Stone. In "Will the Real Body Please Stand Up? Boundary Stories about Virtual Cultures," Stone articulates a reading of cyberspace communities that depicts online identity as an inherently resistant (and mestiza) practice. Taking her cue from Donna Haraway's definition of the cyborg as a border creature, a machine/human construct that challenges dichotomies of identity and carves out new hybrid spaces of being, Stone identifies "those who participate in the 'electronic virtual communities of cyberspace' with the 'boundary-subject' of the Mestiza" (Crane 90). The notion that Internet use alone—considered separately from any other kind of material condition such as interface design, menu structures, and corporate versus independent sponsorship and financing—will create a cyborg or mestiza or, for that matter, anything other than a well-conditioned consumer reflects the state of the Internet in 1991, the year in which Stone's article first appeared. Stone writes, "If the Mestiza is an illegible subject, existing quantum-like in multiple states, then participants in the electronic virtual communities of cyberspace live in the borderlands of both physical and virtual culture, like the Mestiza" (109). Stone is correct to read Anzaldúa's mestiza as an "illegible subject," one that challenges and confounds all simplistic notions of identity. This is precisely why it is impossible for mestiza identity to be expressed in a menu-driven interface; there are no borderlands in portals that require users to click only *one* box to describe something so complex as the "multiple states" occupied by users whose identities are hybrid to any extent. This category would include most users, if we were to get right down to it. Who can—or wants to—claim a perfectly pure, legible identity that can be fully expressed by a decision tree designed by a corporation? This is precisely the sort of empirically driven arrangement that exasperates those of mixed race.

In 1991, cyberspace had yet to be overtaken by advertising, and the web was not yet a dominant interface. The graphic browser had not yet been popularized, and users tended to interact using MOO, chat, and other low-bandwidth programs that permitted only textual interaction. The Net was populated primarily by hobbyists, intellectuals, and academics. In this article, Stone starts off by taking a sustained look at Habitat, an early virtual community in which participants could build and add features to the environment. Most importantly, Habitat was not a moneymaking venture. Thus, the interface might have permitted a sense of "multiple states" of identity that might have created borderlands—spaces of ambiguity or possibility in which identity, racial and otherwise, might be enacted in more free-form, "nonclickable" ways. As Stone notes, these early virtual communities were "incontrovertibly social in character" (90). The notion of the Internet as an unbounded discursive space, a social place where users can build worlds with words, was a fairly short-lived dream.

Why was Stone drawn to the idea of the cyberspace user as mestiza, particularly when "real" mestizas or people of color(s) were so woefully underrepresented in cyberspace at that time as to be nearly entirely absent? Might it have been an attempt to validate and reclaim for the progressive Left what was (and to a large extent still is) an essentially elitist Western practice—computer and Internet use—in 1991? This move colonizes cyberspace in reverse, you might say: it opens up a space for the white computer-using liberal to insert and reenvision herself as other. This is not to claim a position of abjection for its own sake (surely a category to which anyone can aspire via any number of means); rather, it is a way to supplement one's identity prosthesis to make it more . . . *colorful*. Stone does pointedly note that cyberspace isn't purely utopic: "no refigured virtual body, no matter how beautiful, will slow the death of a cyberpunk with AIDS," she writes. "Even in the age of the technosocial subject, life is lived through bodies" (113). When we look at a mestiza in the physical world rather than as a mere figure of speech, symbol or flag of liberation from oppressive binary notions of identity, we can envision her as an actual person who engages with cyberspace in a myriad of materially conditioned ways. It must be acknowledged that the mestiza's affinities for cyberspace have proven to exist more in the realm of academic theory than in the "physical world" of actual Internet usage, where women of color are still underrepresented as both users and producers of web content and interface.

Economic, educational, and cultural inequities amplify the mestiza's difficulties in cyberspace; she is less likely to find the back door into a commercial portal when her access to networked computers is so limited. The "newbie mestiza" who uses the web for the first time is more likely to take Excite's suggestions to "start here," to allow her reading to be guided by an "easy-to-use" portal that then subjects her to its particular hierarchies about race. New users are particularly vulnerable to the ideologies hidden in portals, since successful online services such as America Online have thrived primarily by targeting their products toward inexperienced users who identify themselves as "noncomputer people." As Hoffman and Novak note in their report on the digital divide, African Americans are more likely than whites to identify themselves in this way and thus more likely to rely on a portaled online service, rather than an Internet service provider, as their only means of Internet access from home.

Ultimately, the question of race and its relation to the World

Wide Web boils down to the need for expanded minority access and representation online, as well as critical reexamination of some of the factors that make the web as it exists today an inhospitable place for racial minorities. More minorities need to weave their own webs, webs in which a mestiza or "other" consciousness can become part of the grain rather than always working against it. Websites such as NetNoir and Latino Link do open up spaces for nonwhite users; perhaps most importantly, they foreground racial identity in ways that the vast majority of other commercial websites neglect altogether. These and some other racial- and ethnic-identity websites, many of them created by individuals without corporate affiliations who put up "zines" and other alternative publications expressing their ethnic and racial identities, productively challenge the false but popular and sentimentally utopian notion of cyberspace as raceless. As I will discuss later in this chapter, however, not all ethnic identity websites are created equal: as long as taxonomies of identity are reinforced via interfaces that enforce particular types of choice sets, identity will remain ideologically constrained and informed by an insidious racialism. This type of racialism is often linked to marketing strategies that seek to exploit minorities as the newest "demographic" and to construct them as consumers of information technologies rather than users of a powerful new form of communication and potential community. These sites want to know *what you are* so they can best figure out *what they can sell you.*

The limitations of the web's powers as a force against bigotry and racism are formidable. Until and perhaps even after increased education, economic parity, and changing cultural priorities in the "real world" make the web accessible to a greater number of racial minorities, the medium will reflect the often unconscious racial assumptions and priorities of corporate America. In the meantime, the web has yet to live up to its promise to truly blur the lines between reader and writer, speaker and audience, self and other. We must continue to notice and question what's missing from the various menus offered to us, and work to rewrite these menus in ways that include all of us.

In 2001, Worldcom, a telecommunications company, screened four television advertisements entitled "Refrain," "Thought Bubble,"

"Hosting," and "Simple Cantonese." These ads, part of a series produced in March 2001 entitled "Generation D," (and produced for MCI Worldcom by Messner Vetere Berger McNamee Schmetterer, the same advertising agency that produced the now-famous "Anthem" television ad in 1998 for MCI) are examples of a persistent theme in corporate discourses about new technologies. Rather than "e-rasing" race, the ads employ it as part of a visual strategy, creating an atmosphere of aestheticized and commodified racial diversity; what I would call "Pier One [Imports] Multiculturalism." This spurious diversity so common in 1990s technology advertising raises serious doubts about the potential for digital technologies to foster new, more racially diverse publics (rather than simply new markets).

I do believe that this potential exists, but I don't believe that it is present in the discourse of advertising. Ads like Generation D are very much about sketching out new markets. A more diverse future is in development in cyberspace, but not where you might expect it to be. I see it in more out-of-the-way corners of cyberspace, in e-mail jokes transmitted through personal mailing lists, and so on. If we look at the most low-bandwidth, oldest, and prevalent mode of cyberspatial communication, e-mail, a way of using cyberspace that predates the web by several years (and the one with the shortest learning curve and the greatest accessibility), I argue that we can see online racial and ethnic identities forming in politically progressive ways, ways that reflect some of the lived realities of race offline as well as online. Rather than "brushing race under the mousepad," to use Steven McLaine's memorable phrase (4), these lists and the jokes they circulate inscribe race into cyberspace in collaborative, communal, accessible ways.

The potential of e-mail—an application that is still truly the Internet's "killer app," despite the relatively recent hegemony of the web—to connect users in filiative groups that acknowledge and even critique race in nuanced ways has been more or less ignored in favor of a focus on the web as the dominant means of interacting in cyberspace. This is of no surprise considering the web's influence as a driver of commerce. Yet when we look at many corporate portals, ethnic identity websites, and filmic discourses on race and technology like Generation D, we can see how their interface design and/or content can foster what I call a "menu-driven" notion of racial identity. In this section I want to look under the radar of corporate hype to focus on grassroots uses of joke e-mail lists on the Internet: these lists foster vigorous, sophisticated, self-reflexive, and often hilarious modes of enacting race in cyberspace. The activity of creating or adding to these lists is practically invisible and has no profit motive at all; and anyone who can read and send e-mail can participate. Hence, it fits quite well into an alternative understanding of what racial community on the Internet could and perhaps ought to be. It certainly can be usefully opposed to advertising such as Worldcom's Generation D series.

I chose the Generation D series not because it is weird—though it is—but because it is typical of corporate discourses of race and new communications technology. Though the word *race* is never mentioned in "Refrain," the commercial's dialogue implies its presence fairly heavily, and does depict a rainbow of different skin colors and ethnicities. The narration—"I was born into a new generation . . . Generation D. It isn't about a country, it isn't about a culture, it's about attitude"—is uttered by an attractive Australian woman, one of many pretty people featured in this Benetton-like range of urban cosmopolitan hipsters of color. Unlike their American slacker predecessors in Generation X, the members of Generation D have real jobs (presumably at Worldcom). What's more, they're "reborn" into Generation D; technology here has the effect of stripping them of culture and country, both of which they seem glad to be rid of, replacing national and racial identity with a purely corporate identity. This ad displays race only to subsume it under a corporate identity. These technopeople of color are the ones who make technology "easy to understand." They are the mediators between the benighted hordes of the nondigital and the digerati: their color distinguishes them as appropriate facilitators of intercultural software handshaking, so to speak. If you want assurances that corporate discourses are very much preoccupied with the packaging and reselling (rather than the e-rasure) of race as an adjunct to technology, you've come to the right place: Generation D. Many interesting things vis-à-vis race are happening in this mininarrative: the vision of an Asian-American woman with multiple pigtails asserting (with a Southern accent) that she is from Oklahoma is followed by a shot

of a young blond man who repeats, incredulously, to the camera,
"Oklahoma!" (It appears that he has just had his first encounter
with an Asian American and is still recovering from the experience.)

Here the notion that one could *look* "foreign" yet be American is
seen as more far-fetched than the idea that all these disparate faces,
bodies, voices, languages, and accents could belong to the *same*
generation—Generation D. It is telling that the logic of the ad has
more trouble depicting a "hyphenated American" than an African,
a German, or a Chinese, especially since most high-tech firms, particularly those on either coast, employ Asian Americans on a regular basis. (Indeed, they are the only American racial minority group
with a foot in this particular door.) This Asian American woman's
cultural hybridity has to be foregrounded as such in this discourse
in order to demonstrate both the inclusivity of Worldcom's corporate culture (even "hyphenated Americans" can be—after a bit of
confusion, struggle, and incredulity—successfully assimilated and
co-opted here) and to reinforce racial difference: in the end, what
you see is *not* what you get. Nonetheless, the commercial assumes
that the viewer would be surprised by this difference. For example,
the man who repeats "Oklahoma!" does so in such a way that you
can tell that he still doesn't quite believe it.

Just as clickable menus "drive" race on the web in particular di-
rections and configurations, permitting some categories while entirely eliding or ignoring others, so too has American culture
generally endorsed a very selective set of menus to describe race. As
Gregory Stephens asserts in *On Racial Frontiers: The New Culture
of Frederick Douglass, Ralph Ellison, and Bob Marley,* "If our notions of 'race' have been *invented,* or constructed, out of a repression of the interracial, then the very legitimacy of 'racial' categories
must be questioned" (x). He goes on to point out how "the 'dominant racial mythology' leads biracial or multiethnic individuals to
define themselves in mono-racial or mono-ethnic terms" (3). It is
certainly plausible to read websites that create race-regulating hierarchical menus as lineal descendants of the "dominant racial
mythology" that has enforced such taxonomical sleights of hand as
the famed "one drop" rule for determining the race of interracial
peoples of partially African descent.[7] It is also important to point
out that these taxonomies can often be internalized and enforced by

the very people they are designed to imprison in a racial "box":
Stephens notes that

> the most virulent opposition to the notion that people of
> mixed race can carve out an identity that is neither black nor
> white is now coming from Afro-Americans. Mixed-ethnicity
> children who do not have a black parent are not subject to
> the same "one drop" rule, but for those with a black parent,
> there is often intense pressure to "cleave to the black" and
> accusations of racial betrayal if the individual chooses not to
> choose to be "only black." (33)

Stephens's work makes no reference to the Internet, but his discussion of the historical development of racial taxonomies in the
United States that suppress interraciality and interethnicity as vi-
able identity choices in the service of enforcing more rigid definitions of race bears directly on issues of interface design and identity
construction in cyberspace. When race is put on the menu, as we
shall see shortly in my discussion of ethnic identity websites such as
AsianAvenue.com and BlackPlanet.com, it is cybertyped in such a
way that mestiza or other culturally ambiguous identities—such as
those belonging to hyphenated Americans—are rendered unintelligible, inexpressible, and invisible, since they can't be (or rather,
aren't) given a "box" of their own. Indeed, the fears that their ex-
pression might invalidate "the legitimacy of racial categories," as
Stephens puts it, account for their continued repression in that most
theoretically "free" of all spaces—cyberspace. In the world of the
contemporary interface, if it can't be clicked, that means that it
functionally can't exist.

This suppression of the unclickable, hyphenated, hybrid,
"messy" kinds of racial, gendered, and sexual identity in web interfaces is symptomatic and expressive of, among other things, a long-
standing suspicion of Asian Americans as not *really* American. As I
have pointed out in earlier sections of this book, "pure," authentic
racial identities, preferably exotic ones that are attractive to identity
tourists, are much more serviceable to cyberspace's current ideologies than are racial identities that challenge notions of purity.
Samurai, geishas, and ninjas are romantic images of the Orient that

are fun to acquire and "play" with: images of Asian Americans, especially those from more obscure and economically disadvantaged
ethnic groups such as the Hmong or Lao, are harder to fit into narrative "scripts" that provide a sense of adventure and mastery. The
Asian American presents an additional threat, in the sense that he is
both far away and too close, he is neither really exotic enough to be
commodified by cyberspace's identity markets as "Asian," nor is he
really "American." Poised between these two boxes, so to speak, he
embodies the *contradictions* of Asian immigration, which at different moments in the last century and half of Asian entry into the
United States has placed Asians 'within' the U.S. nation state, its
workplaces, and its markets, yet linguistically, culturally, and
racially [has] marked Asians as 'foreign' and 'outside' the national
polity" (Lowe 8). Certainly, Asian Americans loom large as cyberspace's workers.

AsianAvenue.com, a corporate ethnic identity website, shows
how some of cyberspace's interfaces enforce and cordon off Asian
Americans as permanently "foreign." The site is constructed specifically *for* the Asian/Asian-American user; an examination of it will
highlight the ways that its interface design as much—or in this
case, *more* than—its content determines how menu-driven racial
identities are created and perpetuated.

The site requires users to register by navigating through a series
of clickable menus. After you've chosen your user name and password, you are given seven lists of choices: *ethnicity, lifestyle, music
tastes, news, sports, arts,* and *recreation and hobbies.* Under *ethnicity,* there are nineteen menu choices: Burmese, Cambodian, Chinese, Filipino, Hmong, Indian, Indonesian, Japanese, Korean,
Laotian, Malay, Pacific Islander, Pakistani, Singaporean, Tai-
wanese, Thai, Vietnamese, and "Other." Nowhere is there a box for
"hyphenated" identities. It seems that the concept of the Asian
American is just as impossible or improbable in this theoretically
more ethnically diverse corner of cyberspace as it is in the Worldcom "Generation D" commercials. I say *improbable* because the
last choice on the list is "Other." In fact, the menu does urge the
user to "click all that apply" of the nineteen possible ethnic identities listed; it just so happens that "American" is not one of the
choices. The sense that Asian Americans are too hard to fit into

menu-driven identities is clearly evident in webpages like these. In fact, this difficulty is reflected in the most recent U.S. Census, the first to allow the category "multiracial" onto its menus. The very notion of racial hybridity, what Gregory Stephens dubs the "racial frontier," resists menu-driven identities. This is by no means a new revelation, for anthropologists have been calling for an end to menu-driven means of defining racial identity for years. As Stephens notes, "The American Anthropological Association has called for the elimination of racial categories by the 2010 census" (1).

Even more disturbingly, AsianAvenue.com, BlackPlanet.com, and MiGente.com (three fairly high-profile ethnic identity websites that are all run by Community Connect) have "registration processes [that] have produced a veritable goldmine of niche marketing information. In 1998, Community Connect Inc. estimated that Asians, African Americans, and Latinos together make up one third of the U.S. population and possess nearly $1 trillion in purchasing power" (McLaine 14). McLaine goes on to note his dismay at discovering that the information gathered to fuel what the company calls its "tribal" marketing strategy was readily available on Community Connect's website:

> I was both amazed and disappointed to visit the Community Connect Inc. website and see statistics on all of the members of AsianAvenue.com—broken out by the information I had just provided in registering weeks ago. Neatly compiled and presented for potential clients were percentages of AsianAvenue.com residents by gender, age, lifestyle, income, and state of residence. (McLaine 14)

It appears that it's not only older taxonomies of racial identity that inform menu-driven racial identities; the need for precisely targeted demographic data, strategic advertising campaigns, and "tribal marketing" (a disturbingly colonial locution for describing the best way to sell beads to the natives) also drives the selections available in the "ethnicity" interface. The best way to sell is to know who your client is in the most empirical and quantifiable (or clickable) way possible. And as the gravy train days of venture-capital-driven dot-com growth comes to a close, competition for advertising data becomes all the more intense. Menu-driven interfaces that force users to choose their ethnicity from a limited range of overly simplistic selections define people of color online as "niche markets" (albeit potentially powerful ones). As McLaine notes, this is all the more disappointing in sites that purport to be "ethnic online communities."

This is not to say that corporate-produced websites are always "bad" and grassroots ones are always "good." For example, Net-Noir, one of the oldest and best-established independent African-American-identity websites, recently received corporate backing. This website started out as an independent bulletin board and has thus far retained the sense of community that it started with.

The kind of menu-driven racial identities encouraged in AsianAvenue.com and the census contrast strongly with the e-mail joke lists that I mentioned earlier in this chapter in terms of both content and dynamics of their electronic transmission through cyberspace. Over the last few years I've been archiving Japanese American "joke" e-mails that I receive from my siblings and other Japanese American (JA) friends. I've received one of these, entitled "101 Ways to Tell if You're Japanese American," at least four times from different people! As a result, I have always wanted to amend this list to include an additional 102nd entry to the list: "You can tell you're Japanese American if you forward this list on to all the Japanese Americans you know who have e-mail." Here is the list in its entirety:

1. You know that Camp doesn't mean a cabin in the woods.
2. The men in your family were gardeners, farmers or produce workers.
3. The women in your family were seamstresses, domestic workers, or farm laborers.
4. Your Issei grandparents had an arranged marriage.
5. One of your relatives was a "picture bride."
6. You have Nisei relatives named Keiko, Aiko, Sumi or Mary.
7. You have Nisei relatives named Tak, Tad, George, Harry or Shig.
8. You're Sansei and your name is Janice, Glen, Brian, Bill or Kenji.

9. You're thinking of naming your Yonsei child Brittany, Jenny, Lauren, Garrett or Brett with a Japanese middle name.
10. All of your cousins are having *hapa* kids.
11. You have relatives who live in Hawaii.
12. You belong to a Japanese credit union.
13. Your parents or grandparents bought their first house through a *tanomoshi*.
14. The bushes in your front yard are trimmed into balls.
15. You have a *kaki* tree in the backyard.
16. You have at least one bag of *sembei* in the house at all times.
17. You have a Japanese doll in a glass case in your living room.
18. You have a *Nekko* cat in your house for good luck.
19. You have large Japanese platters in your china cabinet.
20. You have the family *mon* and Japanese needlepoint on the wall.
21. You own a multicolored lime green polyester patchwork quilt.
22. Your grandma used to crochet all your blankets, potholders and dishtowels.
23. You check to see if you need to take off your shoes at your JA friends' houses.
24. When you visit other JAs, you know that you should bring *omiage*.
25. When you visit other JAs, you give or receive a bag of fruits or vegetables.
26. When you leave a JA house, you take leftover food home on a paper plate or a styrofoam meat tray.
27. You keep a supply of rubber bands, twist ties, butter and tofu containers in the kitchen.
28. You have an air pump thermos covered with lilacs.
29. You've heard Warren Furutani speak at least once, somewhere.
30. You've been to the Manzanar Pilgrimage and danced the "*Tanko Bushi.*"
31. Wherever you live now, you always come home to the *Obon* festival in your old neighborhood.
32. You know that Pat Morita doesn't really speak like Mr. Miyagi.
33. You're mad because Kristi Yamaguchi should have gotten more commercial endorsements than Nancy Kerrigan.

34. You know someone who has run for the Nisei Week Queen Pageant.
35. The Japanese American National Museum has asked you for money.
36. If you're under 20, the first thing you read in the *Rafu Shimpo* is the Sports Page.
37. If you're over 60, the first thing you read in the *Rafu Shimpo* is the obituary column.
38. When your back is sore, you use *Salonpas*, Tiger Balm or that flexi-stick with the rubber ball on the end that goes *katonk, katonk.*
39. You've played basketball in the Tigers Tournament.
40. You love to shop at Fedco.
41. You've bowled at the Holiday Bowl, or at least eaten there.
42. You've been to the Far East Café at least once.
43. You've eaten at Mago's or Kenny's Café on Centinela.
44. After funerals, you go for *Chinameshi.*
45. After giving *koden*, you get stamps in the mail.
46. You fight fiercely for the check after dinner.
47. You've hidden money in the pocket of the person who paid for dinner.
48. You don't need to read the instructions on the proper use of *hashi.*
49. You know that Benihana's and Yoshinoya Beef Bowl aren't *really* Japanese food.
50. You eat *soba* on New Year's Eve.
51. You start off the New Year with a bowl of *ozoni* soup for good luck and the *mochi* sticks to the roof of your mouth.
52. You know not to eat the tangerine on top of the mochi at New Year's.
53. You have a 12-pack of mochi in your freezer—that you still refuse to throw away in July.
54. You pack *bento* for road trips.
55. You know that the last weekend in April is Opening Day at Crowley Lake.
56. You stop at Manzanar on the way to and from Mammoth.
57. You see your relatives at the California Club in Las Vegas more often than you see them in L.A.

58. *Your* grandma made the best *sushi* in town.
59. You cut all your carrots and hot dogs at an angle.
60. You know the virtues of SPAM.
61. You were eating Chinese chicken salad, years before everyone else.
62. You know what it means to eat "footballs."
63. You grew up eating ambrosia, *wontons* and finger Jell-O at family potlucks.
64. You always use Best Foods mayonnaise and like to mix it with shoyu to dip broccoli.
65. You use the "finger method" to measure the water for your rice cooker.
66. You grew up on rice: bacon fried rice, chili rice, curry rice or red rice (*osekihan*).
67. You like to eat rice with your spaghetti.
68. You like to eat your rice in a *chawan*, not on a plate.
69. You can't start eating until you have a bowl of rice.
70. You use plastic Cool Whip containers to hold day-old rice.
71. Along with salt and pepper, you have a *shoyu* dispenser at your table.
72. You have a jar of *takuan* in your fridge.
73. You buy rice 25 pounds at a time and shoyu a *gallon* at a time.
74. Natto: you either love it or you hate it.
75. As a kid, you used to eat Botan rice candy.
76. You know the story of *Momotaro*—the Peach Boy.
77. You have had a pet named Chibi or Shiro.
78. Someone you know owns an Akita or Shiba dog.
79. You went to J-school and your best subject was recess.
80. At school, you had those Hello Kitty pencil boxes and sweet smelling erasers.
81. When you're sick, you eat *okayu*.
82. Milk makes you queasy and alcohol turns your face red.
83. Your dad owns a Members Only jacket.
84. Someone you know drives an Acura Integra, Honda Accord, or Toyota Camry.
85. You used to own one of those miniature *zori* keychains.
86. You have a kaeru frog or good luck charm hanging in your car.
87. Your parents compare you to their friends' kids.

88. You hang on to the illusion that you are superior to other Asians.
89. Your dentist, doctor, and optometrist are Japanese American.
90. You know what "S.J." stands for.
91. You socialize with groups of eight or more people.
92. Whenever you're with more than three people, it takes an hour to decide where to eat.
93. You and your friends call yourselves "Buddhaheads," but don't like it when white people do.
94. You've heard your name pronounced a half-dozen different ways.
95. You use the derogatory terms *Kuichi* and *Kurombo* when you should be using *Jewish* and *African American* or *black*.
96. You know what the acronyms M.I.S., 100th/442nd, J.A.C.L., C.Y.C., N.A.U., S.E.Y.O. and S.C.N.G.A. stand for.
97. The name Lillian Baker makes your fists clench.
98. You know that E.O. 9066 isn't a zip code.
99. You're not superstitious, but you do believe in *bachi*.
100. You never take the last piece of food on a plate—but will cut it into smaller pieces.
101. As much as you want it, never ever take the last—anything. *Enryo, enryo, enryo.*

In contrast to AsianAvenue.com and the Generation D commercials, this list defines Asian American identity as irremediably hybrid, various, and "unclickable." It addresses the reader as "you" and provides examples of cultural practices that are paradigmatically "Japanese American," but also supplies plenty of room for readers to display an imperfect or incomplete "ethnic competence," perhaps in itself a "way to tell that you're Japanese American" (or any other kind of ethnic American). As my sister—who was one of many who included me on her mass recipient list for this e-mail—noted, nobody among all her large numbers of Japanese American friends "got" all of these references. This highlights the partial nature of ethnic identification and the degree to which it is always constructed, contingent, and dynamic.

Many of these entries are humorous, but mingled among them are the more overtly political ones, such as: "You know that Camp

doesn't mean a cabin in the woods"; "You hang on to the illusion
that you are superior to other Asians"; and "You use the derogatory
terms *Kuichi* and *Kurombo* when you should be using *Jewish* and
African American or *black*." These entries make specific reference
to Japanese Americans as both the recipients of and perpetrators of
racial prejudice. The recognition of racial as well as cultural hybridity as an infixed aspect of "Japanese Americanness" is evident
in entry number 10: "All your cousins are having *hapa* [half Japan-
ese] kids." The acknowledgment of the role of hybridity in JA identity is referenced in this list—which is itself all about *defining* JA
identity, making for a more flexible notion of race than is possible
in menu-driven cyberspatial media. The list manages to have its
cake and eat it too: it defines racial and ethnic identity in a way
that exemplifies Gayatri Spivak's notion of "strategic essentialism."
As Lisa Lowe puts it,

> The concept of 'strategic essentialism' suggests that it is pos-
> sible to utilize specific signifiers of racialized ethnic identity,
> such as 'Asian American,' for the purpose of contesting and
> disrupting the discourses which exclude Asian Americans,
> while simultaneously revealing the internal contradictions
> and slippages of 'Asian American' so as to insure that such
> essentialisms will not be reproduced and proliferated by the
> very apparatuses we seek to disempower. (82)

This list exploits "specific signifiers" of JA identity partly for the
purposes of humor, but also, more to the point, in order to "hail"
Japanese American–identified readers in cyberspace via discursive
channels. Even more importantly, it is the means of this list's circulation and transmission via cyberspace's e-mail rhizomes or informal networks that puts into relief the ways that it can disrupt
reductive "essentialisms" regarding race and ethnicity. The specific
ways that this list is distributed, via individuals' alias batch e-mail
programs, demonstrates an essentialism that is truly strategic in the
sense that it limns out a kind of racial and ethnic identity grounded
in lived practice but expressed at times as stereotypes while simultaneously challenging definitions of what it means to be Japanese
American, or any other type of "hyphenated" or racially/culturally

mixed person. In this instance, cyberspace becomes a means for "race" to circulate in more subtle and nuanced ways than is possible at times in offline settings.

As I mentioned earlier, I've received this list more than a few times via e-mail. Passing on jokes is a very common practice in cyberspace: users were doing it long before the first graphic web browsers came into being, and such practices persist to this day. My experience as a repeat recipient of this list is not unusual; it's common for users who have been on the Net for a while and who have extensive e-mail traffic to receive the same joke several times from different friends. However, some of these "joke" narratives are identity oriented or race oriented, and construct a racial identity online in a genuine way, a complicated and nuanced way that a hierarchical menu could never convey. What's more, they promote a selectively rhizomatic circulation of identity narratives, weaving multiple and at times recursive connections between people who may or may not actually be, in this case, Japanese American. Here, cyberspace's potential to divorce race, or at least raced narratives, from the body can come true in ways that are actually militated *against* in other cyberspatial media, such as online chat or ethnic-identity websites. The branching paths of racial identity group mail's recipient lists reveal the ways that essentialist notions of Japanese Americanness are regularly challenged and deconstructed by users who seem to be totally unaware of the radical nature of their practice as nodes in an e-mail rhizome.

I interviewed two Asian American women who had sent me this list on separate occasions and asked them to trace its transmission through the electronic sphere. I wanted to know how they decided who among their friends to send it to, and what informed their choices. This question was occasioned by my having noticed a striking fact: many of the names on the list, which was often several dozen names long, were European rather than Japanese. When I asked about this, the senders noted that they sent the list to half-Japanese American (or hapa) and even non-Japanese friends who could "appreciate" it rather than only to "full" JAs. Here, the term *appreciation* implies a kind of ethnic competence that transcends race as biologically understood: anyone who could understand the cultural referents in this list was deemed qualified to receive it. This divorces the idea of Japanese Americanness from notions of racial purity or singularity that are enforced by the hierarchical "pick one" menus of identity such as on Excite or AsianAvenue.com's sites. Instead, it replaces the notion of racial purity with the idea of cultural affinity; Japanese Americanness becomes a series of *situated knowledges* (indeed, the list comes in at least two versions: Southern California and Northern California), to use Donna Haraway's term.[8] This is knowledge that one can only get in the world from being JA, or to some extent JA *identified*. This latter distinction is an important form of hybridity: *hapa* or half-Japanese, comprise a large portion of the list, and being married to or partnered with a JA also qualifies a person for inclusion. My sister (who was one of my informants) has her husband on her recipient list of JA-identity e-mails because he has, for the last several years, spent time living in the world as her partner; attending Obon festivals; hearing my family's identity narratives about visiting Heart Mountain internment camp; never eating the last piece of food on a plate; and fighting over the check. Indeed, he has fought over the check with us and knows how bitter a battle it can be.

He "gets" this list because of his lived relation to and affinities with a Japanese-American family; he has elected to immerse himself in the culture. His constituting a node on the rhizomatic tendrils of this list's journeys through cyberspace actually works to cement that interpolation of the "mainstream" into an American minority culture, and to encourage a kind of multiculturalism that is deinstitutionalized and linked to lived experience. This is an excellent example of an informal, grassroots use of communications technology to create a sense of racial identity that is flexible, hybrid, and de-essentializing. It accomplishes, at least in part, the charge that many of cyberspace's original utopians predicted the Internet would fulfill—that is, to define race in such as way as to detach it from the body. Here, Asian bodies are not appropriated, or bought and sold like Barbie dolls in an avatar boutique for identity tourists, but rather linked to an appreciation of specifically raced narratives; if you "get" it, you are functionally—at least in the moment that you are reading it and "appreciating" it—defined by the list as "knowing you are Japanese American." The list gives you 101 chances to be "in" this identity, and since *nobody but nobody* gets every single one, it evaluates racial and ethnic competence as always the result of a partial, incomplete knowledge rather than the possession of a body that is definitely raced as Asian. The title of the list implies that possession of this knowledge in some way *makes* the reader a Japanese American, if it wasn't "evident" before. This is a crucial formulation, especially for hapa readers, or white partners of JAs, who will eventually be the parents of hapa children. For these users, being Japanese American may be a problematic or liminal subject position. When they receive this list they are being interpellated into a racial identity search engine of sorts that accommodates—indeed, welcomes—their hybridity.

Thus a new sort of racial identity online, one without identity tourism, "eating the other," or cybertyping, is created. This list, which originally appeared in print in the Japanese American newspaper *Rafu Shimpo* in 1996, is also available on several personal webpages, but it seemed important to focus on its circulation via e-mail: for when a user receives it, it "hails" him individually as raced, as "Japanese American." However, it does so in such a way as to strategically challenge the essentialist notion of what that race identification might constitute, since plenty of the people who receive this e-mail are conventionally defined in the world as "white," "interracial," or just plain "other."

It is important to note that despite the dominance of the web, most users still do read their e-mail *before* they perform any other functions on the Internet. In that sense, e-mail is the primal screen/scene of cyberspatial narrative consumption and creation. E-mail is that most low-tech of Internet technologies. While websites become ever more elaborate and feature-packed as broadband infrastructure—such as Ethernet, cable modems, and DSL— become more readily available, they allow for features such as animated films and sound (much of which chiefly serves to enable new and more intrusive forms of advertising). In contrast, e-mail has remained substantially the same since the early 1990s; it has a famously shallow learning curve and is the first application that "newbies" learn to use. It's the original authoring tool. Users who will never acquire the desire or cultural capital to learn hypertext mark-up language, much less high-end and expensive multimedia authoring tools such as Photoshop, Flash, or Director, will express their subjectivity on the Internet as senders and resenders of e-mail. E-mail could be understood to have less of an impact upon the Net since it creates "private" documents (in contrast to websites, which are public). However, this public/private dichotomy breaks down once a closer look is taken at the actual usage practices of e-mail forwarders, many of whom start rhizomatic threads that will eventually reach people who are "strangers."

Can racial identity group mail construct and promote that much-coveted theoretical commodity, an Anzalduan mestiza consciousness? I would contend that it can. First, the content of the JA list cited here is already about defining a hybrid identity, at least culturally; it refers not to knowledge about Japan, but rather to uniquely American practices and landmarks as experienced by a racial minority group. In addition, it is quite possible that a mestiza user could receive several identity-oriented e-mails such as this one in her inbox, all of which, when read in dialogue with each other, would express the complexity of racial, ethnic, class, and gender identities. For example, the "You Know You're a Redneck If . . ." and "Only a Black Woman!" lists (which as far as I can tell tend to circulate via e-mail in the same identity-oriented rhizomatic way as the JA list) could occupy the same space on the screen as multiple identity narratives of this kind.[9] And of course, it's not just race that defines identity. Identities are multivalent: race happens *with* gender, *with* class, *with* sexuality, *with* region.

Little critical attention has been paid to ethnic identity joke group mail, perhaps because it is so low bandwidth, so common a practice. Efforts to incorporate racial minorities as "power users," to bridge the "digital divide" by helping them to start businesses online, acquire faster and more sophisticated machines, and become better consumers of online retailing all too often overlook the more humble types of access that aren't yet, or cannot be, profit making. Nobody makes money off of e-mail; despite the efforts of advertising "spammers" and mass mailers, e-mail is a place in cyberspace that is relatively free of corporate associations. A critical examination of cyberspatial practices that come in under the radar of public and theoretical scrutiny at least tries to honor and acknowledge the racial minority participation that *does* exist on the Internet rather than immediately bemoaning it as inadequate, thus buying into the rhetoric of the digital divide as having a "wrong" or "right" side. Rather than conceiving of narrative practices in cyberspace as if they were old-fashioned literary categories, consisting of "high" (canonical) forms (such as the epic, the lyric poem, the handcrafted website with onboard Java applets, sound, and moving images) versus the "low" (popular) forms (the detective novel, the cartoon, the e-mail message), we would do better to look at rhetorical issues such as audience appropriateness, accessibility, and modes of transmission. To do otherwise is to create hierarchies of privilege that can only misserve cyberspace's newcomers (who are often people of color), thus creating a new kind of cybertyping.

These lists are all about roots: the way that people of color use cyberspace to sustain discourse *about* ourselves *to* ourselves *about* our roots. It's significant that the 120th entry on the "You Know You're Lao If . . ." list is "If you are interested in anything Lao on the Internet." This acknowledges the power that the Internet has as a search engine for racial identity. What's more, the identities that these lists limn out are not corporate, but human, often humorous, ones.

This list and others like it show the dynamic nature of racial formations, the ways in which technology can be understood as just another aspect of racial identity, rather than vice versa. This is absolutely crucial work, for so much corporate and popular discourse exploits race as a way to sell technology, to make it exotic yet familiar at the same time. The "Eighty-two Ways to Tell if You Are Chinese" list has as entry number 65, "You e-mail your Chinese friends at work, even though you only sit 10 feet apart." While the rhetoric of Generation D attempts to subsume race to technology, Internet use in the "You Know You're Lao" and "You Know You're Chinese" lists is figured as just one out of a possible 160 ways of "being Lao" or "being Chinese" rather than as constituting a membership or rebirth into a cultureless place called Generation D, where none of it matters anymore. It turns the tables by casting technology use as one of many aspects of racial identity and practice, rather than vice versa.

While in the Worldcom commercial race/culture/ethnicity has all been shunted aside in favor of a glossy corporate look (the Banana Republic/Benetton model of ethnic chic), these lists reflect the grittier, dorkier, *situated* (in Donna Haraway's sense of the word) side of ethnic identity, visible in examples from the "You Know You're Lao" list: "You had a bowl cut before"; "You know someone who doesn't have a job and is on welfare but still can pay cash for a brand new Toyota 4-Runner"; "Your dad has only one suit and wears it to all occasions"; "You dried your clothing on the back fences of your home"; and "You get nothing if you do well in school, but crapped on if you don't."

As an anonymous sender added as a preface to the "You Know If You're Ghetto" list, "some of these are just for fun, but a lot of them are true." If we look to menu-driven clickable identities on corporate websites, both on "ethnic online communities" and "nonethnic" portals like Excite, what we find are visions of race that are neither fun nor true. It is when we look in the everyday spaces of ethnic participation and racial self-definition by both racial minorities and members of racial-affinity communities such as those created by these joke lists, we can find both the pleasure and pain of being raced in cyberspace.

It is common to visit a website and encounter a sign that reads "under construction." This sign, which often resembles a yellow and black roadsign that you'd see on the highway, warns the viewer that the site you're viewing is not complete, that things will most likely look different, perhaps quite different, the next time you visit. Race *is* under construction in cyberspace. And perhaps this is the best thing that can be said about it. As long as it is still in process, the possibility that it not foreclose ways of being raced that can't be shut up into boxes and clicked as menu choices (and subsequently sold to advertisers) still exists. "Under construction" at least implies that the ways that race is done in cyberspace can change, that new interfaces can come into being that challenge the web monoculture. As the film *The Matrix* figures it, cyberspace itself is a "construct," a constructed environment that we can shape and change after we have "freed our minds" (of racism, among other things). *The Matrix*'s vision of a rebellious multiculture, literally living in the cracks or sewers of a machine-made monoculture, holds out the promise that humans, in all our messy, hybrid, racial diversity, can somehow find a way to resist the categories that pit us against each other, and even, at times, against ourselves.

Lisa Lowe's stated goal in *Immigrant Acts* is to use her critical writing to participate in the "ongoing work of transforming hegemony" (83). Cyberspace's interfaces are perfectly hegemonic, in the sense that they are enforced and informed by dominant ideologies, however unconscious, as well as, to a much lesser extent, infrastructure and design limitations. Lowe's faith that hegemony *can* be transformed through critical endeavors as well as through direct and indirect forms of political activism is one that we must take with us into future cyberspaces, just as we must continue to look for resistances and insistences on the particularity, complexity, and lived experiences of racial identity in the Internet's more out-of-the-way places. It is naive to expect that corporations and the mainstream media complex will produce the kind of interfaces or content that reflect a noncommodified style of racial diversity. The burden and privilege of creating racial and ethnic community in cyberspace must be taken up by critics, artists, users, and designers of color before the master's tools can be used to dismantle the master's house.

<CONCLUSION>

KEEPING IT (VIRTUALLY) REAL: THE DISCOURSE OF CYBERSPACE AS AN OBJECT OF KNOWLEDGE

The Internet, like hip-hop, came up in the mid-1990s as a cultural force to be reckoned with, as well as a newly anointed object of academic study.[1] And as new objects of knowledge and institutions, both are struggling with questions regarding legitimacy, identity politics, and disciplinary boundaries. In the case of hip-hop, these struggles have been loud and well documented; the question of who has the authority to use the form, who consumes it and in what fashion, has always been discussed with reference to racial positioning, as it ought to be. Hip-hop's subversive potential as a medium that gives voice to African American and Latino artists disenfranchised from power by the prison industrial complex is inseparably tied to its roots in lived experience, specifically in experiences of racism. However, in the case of cyberculture studies, these struggles have been practically invisible. Perhaps this is in part due to the rhetoric of cyberspace itself, which proclaims the Internet to be above all a democratic space, one that promises to provide everyone with access to the articulation of self within the public—even global—sphere. Nonetheless, it is precisely because cyberspace studies have, in the short lifespan of five years, consistently overlooked, elided, and just plain ignored race and racialism that they bear examining today. I will herein examine the institutional, ideological, and political reasons for this omission, as well as identify some ways in which the academic study of the Internet might "keep it real" in the culture of simulation.

At first glance the omission is puzzling indeed, for, as Anne duCille writes, we are living in a moment in American studies where "within the modern academy, racial and gender alterity has become a hot commodity." The study of "subjugated subjects" or "peasants under glass," as she so vividly puts it, has become more than fashionable; it has become practically de rigueur in some fields, particularly in postcolonial and ethnic literature. Given this, one might expect cyberculture studies to follow this disciplinary trend, yet thus far they have resisted it. While studies of previously marginalized issues such as race and gender in literature, film, and other media have proven extremely attractive (to duCille, disturbingly so), to white male and female academics, studies of race—and to a lesser extent, ethnicity—in cyberculture have not. Why is this?

To answer this question, it is crucial to address additional questions, such as, Who gets to speak about cyberspace? Who gets to speak *in* cyberspace? Who *wants* to speak *about* it? Who is trained to produce scholarly work in cyberculture? What kind of scholarly work has shaped the field today, such as it is? Are there racial "digital divides," or institutionalized inequities in access, resources, and cultural/academic capital, that obtain both inside cyberspace and in the field of cyberculture studies? Whose ideas have power? Whose discourse is privileged? And why haven't these questions been asked before?

It is only within the last five years or so that cyberculture studies have become an academic field or an object of knowledge; 1995 was a watershed year that saw both the irreversible and thoroughgoing popularization of the web and the instantiation of the Internet as a fixture of postmodern life, as well as the publication of some critical academic studies in cyberculture, such as Steve Jones's seminal collection *CyberSociety*. Websites such as David Silver's Resource Center for Cyberculture Studies provide excellent bibliographies of cyberculture scholarship, and attest to the existence of a "there" there, in regard to cyberspace as an object of knowledge and a legitimate—if at times atomized—field of study. What is missing, however, in the scholarship is attention to race as an important component of online identity and community.

Though there is important work being done now on race in cyberspace, it tends to draw attention to the paucity of other work on the topic and makes impassioned pleas for more to be done. As Thomas Foster writes (as recently as 1999), "to date, [. . .] the discourse on cyberspace demonstrates a striking lack of engagement with the possible racial implications of such theoretical work [as Donna Haraway's and Allucquère Rosanne Stone's seminal writings in cyberculture]" (138).[2] And while scholars like Foster, Radhika Gajjala, Rajani Sudan, Kalí Tal, and Ziauddin Sardar have produced important articles on race in cyberspace, there have been heretofore no single-authored book-length studies on the topic. Indeed, Kalí Tal writes in "The Unbearable Whiteness of Being: African American Critical Theory and Cyberculture" that "in cyberspace, it is possible to completely and utterly disappear people of color" and that the elision of questions of race has led to cyberspace's "whitinizing." The same can be said of cyberspace studies.

Again, considering the ways in which cultural studies have generally led to an increased focus on subaltern identities and issues of race and representation, and the fact that many of its scholars, as well as scholars in other fields, are trained in cultural-studies methods and the iterations of race and raciality in media generally, then why the omission? Since cyberculture is such a young field, and the web is effectively only about six years old,[3] everyone doing critical work on the web has had *at most* five years of experience. Studies on preweb Internet media, such as Internet relay chat, multiple user dimensions, and bulletin boards appeared somewhat earlier. This kind of academic environment seems to level the playing field, and as the prominence of articles in cyberspace collections by graduate students attests, cyberculture studies seem to be accessible to scholars who are less established in the academy generally. This would seem to encourage approaches that are apt to interrogate racial identities in cyberspace, yet this has not been the case.

DIGITAL DIVIDES WITHIN ACADEME

I wish to read this state of things in dialogue with another set of material conditions in academe—that is, the underrepresentation of people of color in tenured or tenure-track professorial positions in the humanities. The trope of the digital divide, a much-cited social problem in regard to inequities in online access and access to information technologies in general, obtains in a slightly different form in relation to cyberculture studies. There is indeed a digital divide in cyberculture studies, and, like the digital divide in online access, it is keyed to racial categories. Cyberculture studies is just one of many fields minority scholars are, de facto, steered away from; my intent is to look at the possible effects of this on the field and its discourse. This academic digital divide leads to a lack of voice regarding race and difference online.

Gender online has been examined in depth, but race has not, perhaps reflecting the closing gender gap both in the halls of academe and online. On June 29, 2000, the *New York Times* published research showing that "Web use became balanced for the first time this year with 31.1 million men and 30.2 million women online in April [. . .]. In some months, female users have significantly outnumbered their male counterparts" (Austen D7). In addition, data from the 1999 U.S. Department of Education show that there are now slightly more women getting Ph.D.'s in English than men. However, "newbies" in cyberspace as well as in academia lack full command of the discourse (and thus, power within it), and are less likely to have a hand in shaping it. Just as newbies to the web lack authority and experience in regard to web authorship, creating protocols for usage, and creating a vocabulary or vernacular, so too are newbies in the academy just beginning to wield rhetorical power within it.

When scholars of color are hired, they are often expected to bear the burden of "representativity"—to represent their race in the teaching of minority literatures and culture, which is not (yet) construed to include cyberspace or the Internet. This represents yet another layer of digital and disciplinary divide.[4] Pressures to stay within the already well-delineated (if struggling, during this time of national budget surpluses accompanied by instructional funding cuts) fields of African American literature, Asian American literature, and ethnic or "area" studies result in fewer scholars of color working on cyberculture studies. The pressure on academics of color to stay within their disciplinary "boxes," a condition exacerbated by—in many cases—their being the only instructor "responsible" for these courses, often limits them to teaching and research on "ethnic literatures" and other matters traditionally seen to relate to this field.

Thus, the training in ethnic studies that might lead to more critical and theoretical work on race in cyberspace has been monopolized by the study of ethnic literatures. And, as has also been well documented, the pressure on scholars—particularly untenured female scholars—of color to support ethnic student groups at their home institutions, to appear on panels or as speakers on racial and ethnic issues on campus, and to mentor students in their racial groups with particular vigor, leaves little energy or resources to devote to blazing new trails in a new and as yet untested field.[5] These pressures to create a discourse of racial tolerance and cultural diversity, and to contribute some "flavor" to home institutions, come from within and without, and as such they can be especially compelling and difficult to ignore.

Incentives to keep one's nose to the grindstone of campus climate issues and ethnic studies as they are traditionally conceived work to divert junior faculty of color from new fields like cyberspace studies—particularly when these scholars reside within institutions where cyberculture publications may not be as valued toward earning tenure as other sorts of more "traditional" publications might be. While tenured and secure faculty may take advantage of cyberculture studies as an exciting opportunity to produce a second book on a cutting-edge topic, untenured faculty of color may feel pressure to publish in the fields in which they were hired, which are—by and large—studies of ethnic literature. Cyberculture studies thus functions, at times, as a "second field" for established (read: fully employed and tenured) academics.

Of course, the current dire state of the academic job market has a bearing on these decisions. As Leslie Bow puts it, "How can equity for women of color in the profession appear as a crisis when simply being in the profession is constructed as a privilege?" (220). Given the embattled state of the academy generally, it is not surprising that scholars of color, already expected to wear so many hats in their home institutions, are not turning out in force to contribute their expertise on race to cyberculture studies. A lack of institutional support for this makes it extremely difficult for these scholars to write the kinds of articles that are collected in textbooks, published in refereed journals, and appear on course syllabi.

Needless to say, this conditions the shape of the field's discourse; and here is one of the many paradoxes attendant upon this new field of study: while cyberculture studies occupies what is, in some sense, a privileged position: as "current," on the cutting edge (a case in which the terminology applied to the technology itself is applied to studies *of* the technology), and enjoys some of the high status accorded to information technologies in our culture at present, it is also a young and embattled field, the site of disciplinary struggles, and has yet to find a consistent disciplinary home (courses on the topic are offered in English, rhetoric, communications, and cultural studies departments). The mainstream media's claims that the Internet will (or has) transformed our society in fundamental ways are yet to be fully realized; likewise, the changes wrought upon the academy by cyberspace studies are in process as well. In addition, the stakes around these questions are especially high for academics, as distance learning makes inroads upon our very livelihoods, and we find ourselves forced to make arguments justifying the value of our face-to-face pedagogical interactions with students.

Considering all of this, is it unreasonable to expect cyberculture studies to deal with race? Whether or not the expectation is reasonable, it is certainly possible to speculate about what impact this omission might have on future studies and on the shape of the field generally. What does it mean when we fail to hear the voices of racial minorities in regard to race and cyberculture?

It means a great deal, for cyberspace is a community as well a medium—an interactive social space where race is just as much an aspect of the culture as it is offline. The experience in being a racial minority online is a salient aspect of the "culture" part of "cyberculture." Dana Canady, a staff reporter for the *New York Times*, coined the phrase "black surprise" to describe what happens when informants she has interviewed by phone meet her for the first time and realize that she is black (Roberts 22).

Considering the large numbers of users that avail themselves of chat spaces to interact with others online, the dynamics of "black surprise," or rather the discovery that the interlocutor with whom you are chatting is raced in ways different from those you expected, will become all the more important topics of study as increasing numbers of minority groups get online. Canady writes that "black surprise" changes the social dynamics between her and her informants; in her case, people whom she had had long relationships with via electronic media (i.e., telephones) simply failed to see her when they met "because she was a black person." The culture of simulation engendered by the Internet counts "black surprise" as only one of its many features that will create new discourses of race in cyberspace.

Being "raced" in the context of cyberspace creates knotty methodological issues for cyberculture scholars that can make one's head spin. For example, when I engage in online chat and/or research on Club Connect, am I engaging in "black" discourse if I create a character who self-presents as black and interacts with other characters who appear to be black as well? How would I or others know? Am I part of that community while "in" that character, but not a part of it if I create a new, differently raced character? This example brings up some extremely complex issues regarding authenticity vis-à-vis race—issues that ethnic studies has much to contribute toward.

Because cyberspace is a place where racial identities are created, maintained, received, and performed, a user's position as raced offline counts for something—for most minorities have experienced, at one time or another, something akin to "black surprise" long before the Internet came along. Even before cyberculture studies put forward the notion of identities (including racial identities) as "prostheses," or features to be taken off and put on like new user names, people of color lived it. To be raced in America means to live in a culture of simulation regarding race. As Phillip Brian Harper puts it,

> [I]f postmodernist fiction foregrounds subjective fragmentation, a similar decenteredness can be identified in U.S. novels written prior to the postmodern era, in which it derives specifically from the socially marginalized and politically disenfranchised status of the populations treated in the works. To the extent that such populations have experienced psychic decenteredness long prior to its generalization throughout the culture during the late twentieth century, one might say that the postmodern era's preoccupation with fragmentation represents the "recentering" of the culture's focus on issues that have always concerned marginalized constituencies. (3–4)

Even the most innocuous seeming of cultural practices, such as talking on the phone or shopping by mail order, affords occasions for people of color to slip in and out of interactions where their race is visible or invisible, to experience "psychic decenteredness," to know what it means to live in the shock in between those two polarities. When users go online, race dwells in the mediating space between the virtual and the real, the visible and the invisible; when the line between the two is crossed, disruptive moments of recognition and misrecognition can ensue. Thus, those moments when race enters the picture in multiple-user dimensions and a player's race is discovered to be different from that of his character are politically charged and can offer the opportunity for some critical reassessment of racist assumptions. Perhaps this is one of the most subversive opportunities that cyberculture has to offer us in terms of race: if cross-racial role-playing is able to give white people any sense of what the shock of "racial surprise" feels like, it has the potential to disrupt notions of racial authenticity and identity which may be productive.

As the term *cyberculture* implies, Internet users are seen to engage in a *culture* unto itself, something more inclusive than a single "cultural activity." As in other cultures (women's culture, African American culture, Asian American culture), personal identity and subject positioning count in a way that they don't in other academic "fields." In some ways, cyberculture studies have more in common with Asian American studies or women's studies, where *what you are* (meaning the particular and specific cultural experiences and contexts in which you have experienced life) signifies the ways in which you can articulate yourself in addition to *how you are heard.*

KEEPING IT REAL

As I have tried to demonstrate, the material conditions and dynamics of academic employment in our time, academic identity politics, and disciplinary boundaries regarding "ethnic" studies have militated to keep the numbers of minority scholars writing on race in cyberspace at a minimum. In addition to these conditions, figurations and fantasies of cyberspace as a utopic "raceless place" contribute to the status quo. The Internet is often figured as a refuge from race. a high-tech antidote to "racial fatigue" (Roberts 22).

Even as the Internet makes it increasingly difficult to police the line between the virtual and the "real," it is vitally important for cyberculture studies to "keep it real"—to remember that while race may be, in some sense, "virtual" or at the very least culturally and discursively constructed as opposed to biologically grounded, racism both on- and offline *are* real. The lessons of deconstruction have taught us to look for the silences or omissions in discourse, and the ways in which these erasures and suppressions condition the shape of "truth." When we examine cyberculture studies and notice who is *not* speaking, and those things that are not spoken of, it becomes apparent that race is still the Rubicon that the field has yet to cross. The paucity of scholars of color in the still-developing field, combined with the reluctance to grapple with the knotty issues of racial representation online (such as the ways in which "race" is signified or suppressed in textual and graphical environments) work together to block cyberspace studies from potential avenues of inquiry.

Future cyberculture scholars will look back and acknowledge both the existence of a digital divide in the field and the effects that this had upon the contours of its discourse. And like older academic studies of minorities and language/cultural formations, it will recognize the material conditions that led to this lack, and the discursive formations that came out of it. McKenzie Wark's oft-quoted statement regarding the shift in conceptions of personal and cultural identity symptomatic of the digital age—"We no longer have roots, we have aerials"—posits an end to that sense of rootedness, of positioning in a culture, of facing life in a raced body that ineluctably conditions the lived realities of the vast majority of the world's people. Trading in roots for aerials seems an unequal, unreal proposition considering the glaring inequities in access to the Internet (not to mention wireless communications) that apply to most people of color. Aerials are expensive; cultural capital, actual capital, and access to hardware infrastructures are all part of the price. *Race*, as vexed a term as it has come to be, is an indispensable part of the "root" that warrants, anchors, and conditions the lives of actual users in cyberspace to the world offline. Rather than seeing offline life and life in cyberspace as being two entirely separate spheres, cyberculture studies must examine the "roots" of one within the other—the ways in which racial, gendered, and cultural histories and the identities conditioned by them in turn shape the discourses that are audible in and about cyberspace. Only then can the field begin to claim cyberspace as an object of knowledge in a way that "keeps it real," that resists co-optation by corporate and cultural forces that would curtail its considerable subversive potential in regard to oppressive notions of racial identity.

NOTES

INTRODUCTION

1. The penchant of theory to attach a *post* (like postmodernism and poststructuralism) to movements and theories appears to be alive and well.

2. See James Gleick's book *Faster* for a more sustained discussion of "Internet time" (83).

3. See David Silver's useful formulation regarding the ways that "the digital architecture of an online environment [can] influence or help to determine the kinds of cultural exchanges and interactions that take place" online. When interfaces not only ignore, but rather "route around" issues of race, gender, and sexuality, they "code its participants as the digital default: white, male, and heterosexual" (143).

4. The "recent critics" referred to by Punday are Shannon McRae, Stephen Shaviro, and myself.

5. There is still a huge amount of research to be done in this area: as Punday writes, "in contrast to gender issues, race online has received considerably less attention. When critics do address such issues, the emphasis is usually on access to the Internet rather than on how race is represented" (211).

6. MUDs (multiple-user dimensions, or multiple-user dungeons) and MOOs (multiple-user dimensions, object oriented) are computer programs that numerous users can log into and explore while interacting with each other.

CHAPTER 1: CYBERTYPING AND THE WORK OF RACE IN THE AGE OF DIGITAL REPRODUCTION

1. The amount of scholarship on embodiment and disembodiment in cyberspace is fairly substantial. See N. Katherine Hayles's *How We Became Posthuman* for a trenchant philosophical and literary approach to the issue, as well as Allucquère Stone's *The War of Desire and Technology*. Hayles covers a range of examples of body-technologies, while Stone is more Internet-specific. An article that addresses the issue of race and embodiment in cyberspace via an examination of digital art is Jennifer Gonzalez's "The Appended Subject: Race and Identity as Digital Assemblage."

2. In an article entitled "Survivor: As Internet Industry Plays Survival of the Fittest, Netnoir.com celebrates 5th Anniversary," which appeared in

Netnoir.com's online newsletter in 2000, the company announced that San Francisco mayor Willie Brown had proclaimed June 22 "Netnoir.com day in the city and county of San Francisco." In 1994, Netnoir.com's E. David Ellington received an award from the AOL Greenhouse Project to fund information technology entrepreneurs, and "soon after, AOL backed NetNoir with a 19.9 percent equity stake." Currently, NetNoir has partnered with AOL, Syncom Ventures, and Radio One. NetNoir's slogan—"Taking you there. Wherever there is"—stands as an interesting contrast to Microsoft's "Where do you want to go today?" in the sense that it is far more open-ended about the web's topography and structure.

3. Since the incredible dominance of the Internet by the World Wide Web in the 1990s, it has consistently supported this construction of women *as* bodies. The notion that the Internet is 90 percent pornography and advertising, while it may be a slight exaggeration, gestures toward the Internet's role as an extremely efficient purveyor of exploitative images of women. Similarly, the Internet's current bent toward merchandising and selling online constructs women as either "markets" or more commonly as scantily clad figures in commercials for products.

4. Kozmo.com has since gone out of business, for reasons unrelated to this lawsuit.

5. See *Posthuman Bodies*, edited by Judith Halberstam and Ira Livingston, as well as Scott Bukatman's *Terminal Identity: The Virtual Subject in Postmodern Fiction*.

6. Guillermo Gomez-Peña's work is a notable exception. In *Dangerous Border Crossers*, he describes how responses from live audiences and Internet users became the inspiration for a "series of performance personae or 'ethno-cyborgs' co-created (or rather 'coimagined') in dialogue with gallery visitors and anonymous net users" (49). These ethno-cyborgs are collaboratively constructed by canvassing and melding together Internet users' "projections and preconceptions about Latinos and indigenous people." (46). This performance project, *Mexterminator*, was constructed from the "majority of responses we received [that] portrayed Mexicans and Chicanos as threatening Others, indestructible invaders, and public enemies of America's fragile sense of coherent national identity" (49). Thus, these ethno-cyborgs are synthesized cybertypes of Mexican American identity.

7. Just as computer users become accustomed to the "look and feel" of particular interfaces (the loyalty of Macintosh users to the desktop metaphor is legendary), so too do consumers of popular discourse become strongly attached to particular images of race. As software designers and webmasters have learned, users are quick to protest when familiar websites, such as Amazon.com's, are redesigned, and these designers have often

responded to consumer protests by changing them back to their original appearance. This is also the case for the ways that the "native" is portrayed in popular culture.

8. See Alondra Nelson and colleague's essay collection *Technicolor: Race, Technology and Everyday Life* for a critique of this formulation; their work posits a reframing and redefinition of the "technical" to include sampling, sound technologies, and communications technologies such as the beeper, cellphone, and pager in ways that would "count" African Americans as innovators and users of note.

9. This is akin to Neal Stephenson's cyberpunk novel *The Diamond Age*, which represents Chinese girls as members of a faceless "horde" of model minorities.

10. Growing attention has been paid to the existence of a "glass ceiling" for Asian engineers in the high-technology industry, particularly in Asian-American publications and newspapers. However, despite this glass ceiling, R. Mutthuswami asserts that "highly educated Indians [. . .] serve as CEOs of 25 percent of the companies in Silicon Valley" (quoted in Kumar 81).

11. One can see the headhunter's analogue in the more down-market image of the "coyote." Coyotes are "smugglers of workers and goods . . . for the farms of South Texas, the hotels of Las Vegas and the sweatshops of Los Angeles" (Davis 27). They guide people across the U.S. Mexican border, and there are often casualties along the way.

12. Despite the existence of black-oriented programming on smaller cable networks such as the WB and UPN, the majority of African Americans, as well as Asians and Latinos (groups even less depicted on television as primary characters), understandably feel that their lived realities are entirely unrepresented on television. Of course the same is true for whites: few possess the limitless leisure and privilege enjoyed by the characters on the show *Friends*, for example; but they might at least aspire to these roles. What African-American woman truly would want to be the "hoochie mama" depicted on Rikki Lake's "reality" programming or the noble black mammy Oracle in the film *The Matrix*?

CHAPTER 2: HEAD-HUNTING ON THE INTERNET

1. MUDs (multiple-user dimensions, or multiple-user dungeons) and MOOs (multiple-user dimensions, object oriented) are computer programs that numerous users can log into and explore while interacting with each other. For scholarly analysis of this, see Julian Dibbell's "A Rape in Cyberspace" and *My Tiny Life*, Sherry Turkle's *Life on the Screen*, and several of the articles in the collections *Communities in Cyberspace* (ed. Marc A.

Smith and Peter Kollack) and *The Cybercultures Reader* (ed. David Bell and Barbara M. Kennedy), such as Randal Woodland's "Queer Spaces, Modem Boys, and Pagan Statues," Shawn Wilbur's "An Archaeology of Cyberspaces," in *Cybercultures Reader*, and Jodi O'Brien's "Writing in the Body: Gender [Re]Production in Online Interaction," in *Communities in Cyberspace*. See also Elizabeth Reid's work, especially her essay "Hierarchy and Power: Social Control in Cyberspace," in *Communities in Cyberspace*, and Lynn Cherny's work, in particular *Conversation and Community: Discourse in a Social MUD.*

2. See Haraway 163.

3. Some MUDs, such as Diku and Phoenix, require players to select races. These MUDs are patterned after the role-playing game Dungeons and Dragons and, unlike Lambda, which exists to provide a forum for social interaction and chatting, focus primarily on virtual combat and the accumulation of game points. The races available to players (orc, elf, dwarf, human, etc.) are familiar to readers of the "sword and sorcery" genre of science fiction, and determine what sort of combat attributes a player can exploit. The combat metaphor, which is a part of this genre of role-playing, reinforces the notion of racial difference.

4. Computer users using their machines to play games at work realized that it was possible for their employers and coworkers to spy on them and thus notice that they were slacking off. Hence, they developed screen savers that, at a keystroke, could instantly cover their play with a convincingly worklike image, such as a spreadsheet or business letter.

5. The political action group devoted to defending the right to free speech in cyberspace against governmental control calls itself The Electronic Frontier Foundation. This is another example of the metaphorization of cyberspace as a colony with borders that need to be defended against hostile takeovers.

6. Of course, the nature rather than merely the quantity of online representations of racial minorities is what needs to be considered here. As Mimi Nguyen writes, "If representational visibility equals power, then almost-naked young Asian women should be running a very big chunk of cyberspace. That is, whenever I type 'asian+women' [into a search engine] I get almost nothing but them" (183).

7. See Jeff Ow's article on orientalist yellow-face imagery in video games entitled "The Revenge of the Yellow-Faced Cyborg: The Rape of Digital Geishas and the Colonization of Cyber-Coolies in 3D Realms' Shadow Warrior" published in *Race in Cyberspace* for a notable exception to this rule.

8. Microsoft's and Netscape's web browser programs, entitled Internet Explorer and Navigator, respectively, emphasize the links between the no-

tion of travel and tourism and the graphical web. The web browser which preceded them, Mosaic, was a tool for browsing the web in the days when it was text based; hence its name emphasizes the image of the hyperlinked or fragmented web rather than the notion of the web as a space to be traversed and colonized in a ship. Netscape's Navigator icon features an imperial-era tallship steering wheel, further reinforcing this imagery. I am indebted to Matthew Byrnie for this observation.

9. Souvenirs are trophies that evoke memories of an experience rather than commodities possessing an independent or exchange value (see Mac-Cannell 124).

10. See Sherry Turkle, *Life on the Screen* (13).

11. In his analysis of ethnic identity websites, Steve McLaine observes that it's often users of EOCs, or ethnic online communities, that create screen names for themselves like "blacklatindiva, spicygirl, AlatinoLover [. . .] and hoocheemama" that seem to "freely flaunt stereotypes as identification" (18). McLaine speculates that this may constitute a form of empowerment, of taking back the discourse of oppression and repurposing it as a form of solidarity, as in the use of the word *nigger* by African Americans. In any case, the deployment of these terms by users of any "real life" race or ethnicity demonstrates that race must be cybertyped online to be recognizable. Though it is possible that cybertyping could be used as a means to building race-based communities online, its deployment will always be problematic in the same sense that the use of the word *nigger* is.

CHAPTER 3: RACE IN THE CONSTRUCT AND THE CONSTRUCTION OF RACE

1. This is less the case in the two subsequent volumes in Gibson's *Sprawl* trilogy, *Mona Lisa Overdrive* and *Count Zero*. *Mona Lisa Overdrive*, in particular, features a major Japanese female character. For an excellent article on the function of race in "hacker" films see David Crane's "In Media's Race: Filmic Representation, Networked Communication, and Racial Intermediation."

2. Cyberpunk writers are overwhelmingly white and male, and according to the highly acclaimed African-American science-fiction writer Samuel Delany, mainstream science-fiction's institutions seem to want to keep it that way. In his 1999 essay "Racism and Science Fiction" he writes:

In the days of cyberpunk, I was often cited by both the writers involved and the critics writing about them as an influence. As a critic, several times I wrote about the cyberpunk writers. And Bill

Gibson wrote a gracious and appreciative introduction to the 1996 reprint of my novel *Dhalgren*. Thus you might think that there were a fair number of reasons for me to appear on panels with those cyberpunk writers or to be involved in programs with them [. . .]. Nevertheless: Throughout all of cyberpunk's active history, I only recall being asked to sit on *one* cyberpunk panel with Gibson [. . .] in the last ten years, however, I have been invited to appear with [African-American science-fiction writer] Octavia [Butler] at least six times [. . .]. All the comparison points out is the pure and unmitigated strength of the discourse of race in our country vis-à-vis any other." (396)

3. *The Diamond Age* is particularly problematic in its orientalist depiction of this horde of orphaned Chinese girls who live only to serve their white female leader, Nell. None of these girls has a name: they exist only as "Nell's tribe, and they had come for their leader [. . .]. Nell was being borne on the shoulders of her little sisters out the front doors of the building and into the plaza, where something like a hundred thousand girls— Nell could not count all the regiments and brigades—collapsed to their knees in unison [. . .] all of them bowing to Nell, not with a Chinese bow or a Victorian one but something they'd come up with that was in between" (436). This fantasy scenario recalls much older colonial narratives like the *Tarzan* films, in which white superiority is instinctively acknowledged by appreciative and faceless "natives."

4. The directors' commentary, which comes on the DVD version of *The Matrix*, also omits the topic of race entirely, as do the actors. There are no references to race at all in the wealth of additional and supporting material provided on this state-of-the-art DVD.

5. This is another cautionary reference to the Internet: in 1996, digital agents were celebrated in *Wired* magazine as the next new thing in cyberspace. These software programs were supposed to do the tedious work of searching information out in cyberspace; in this film they've acquired sentience, rebelled, and taken over the system.

6. In the DVD commentary to *The Matrix*, Laurence Fishburne says that "Morpheus is a person who lives in the *real* world."

7. Trinity would seem to be a descendant of Molly, the warrior "razorgirl" in Gibson's *Sprawl* trilogy.

8. Cypher also has a possessive investment in maleness: as he says to Neo while looking at the monitor of coded signs that represent the software of the matrix, "All I see is blonde, brunette, redhead." This is the only invocation of sexist language in a film that depicts women as formidable war-

riors and computer hackers—Trinity is both a fighter and the person who "hacked into the IRS D-base." Part of Trinity's role in the film is to school Neo and the viewer that women can "hack it" too. When Neo comments "I thought you were a man," upon learning of her software expertise, she responds by saying "Most men do," a clever acknowledgment and rebuke of gender stereotypes.

9. See Sherry Turkle, *Life on the Screen: Identity in the Age of the Internet*; Allucquère Rosanne Stone, *The War of Desire and Technology*; Lynn Cherny and Elizabeth Reba Weise, eds., *Wired Women: Gender and New Reality in Cyberspace*; and Thomas Foster, "'Trapped by the Body?' Telepresence Technologies and Transgendered Performance in Feminist and Lesbian Rewritings of Cyberpunk Fiction" for discussions of cross-gender role-playing in cyberspace. See also *Race in Cyberspace*, ed. Beth E. Kolko, Lisa Nakamura, and Gilbert B. Rodman (New York: Routledge, 2000).

10. The term *avatar*, used to describe a visual digital representation of a self in cyberspace, was first coined in popular literature by Neal Stephenson in *Snow Crash*. He writes, "Your avatar can look any way you want it to, up to the limitations of your equipment. If you're ugly, you can make your avatar beautiful. If you've just gotten out of bed, your avatar can still be wearing beautiful clothes and professionally applied makeup" (36).

11. In a *New York Times Magazine* "Fashions of the Times" issue, *The Matrix* is cited, along with the film *Gattaca*, as a "fashion show" (Mitchell) While wardrobe is a necessary component of the visual field that signifies to film viewers that the action is taking place in the future rather than now, the article's author claims that the cutting-edge fashions actually overshadow the plot.

12. When at the beginning of the film Neo is shown extracting black-market recreational software from a hollowed-out book entitled *Simulacra and Simulation*, these issues are being foreshadowed fairly overtly. The reference to Jean Baudrillard's *Simulacra and Simulation* constitutes a broad intertextual wink to the audience, particularly since so many cyberculture theorists like to cite Baudrillard as an influence on their work.

13. The black character Tank, though left for dead by Cypher, does manage to survive and in fact kills Cypher. This allows him to continue as the crew's "operator" and to eventually pull the heroes out of the matrix back into the real world, thus reinforcing the connections the film has built between "raced" characters and the real. However, his role in the film is somewhat effaced; he operates behind the scenes, much like the Oracle, and never participates in any of the telegenic battles with the agents that contain most of the film's narrative high points.

14. It seems that this "open secret" is constructed primarily by viewers'

own residual self-images or identifications; while Asians tend generally to know Reeves's interracial status, whites do not.

15. See Donna Hoffman and Thomas P. Novak, "Bridging the Digital Divide: The Impact of Race on Computer Access and Internet Use," for a discussion and explanation of low usage of the Internet by minorities compared to whites.

16. This is very much a convention of cyberspace narrative since its inception. See Scott Bukatman's *Terminal Identity: The Virtual Subject in Postmodern Science Fiction*.

CHAPTER 4: "WHERE DO YOU WANT TO GO TODAY?"

1. Kaplan writes that in order to address these connections, we must "consider the specifically Euro-American histories of imperialist nostalgia in the construction of modernist exile, constructions that require the conflation of exile, expatriation, and tourism in the representational practices of cultural production" (35).

CHAPTER 5: MENU-DRIVEN IDENTITIES

1. In *Borderlands/La Frontera*, feminist critic Gloria Anzaldúa describes the *mestiza* as "the product of the transfer of the cultural and spiritual values of one group to another" (78). The product of "racial, ideological, cultural and biological cross-pollination" (77), the mestiza is figured by Anzaldúa as a "border" figure, meaning that she signifies the place where cultures, races, and discourses mingle to produce a hybrid type of subject.

2. The use of the term *rhizome* has "become a kind of catchword in cyberspace," (65) according to Douglas Stanley (Nunes 65). The term hearkens to the language of Gilles Deleuze and Félix Guattari, who make the distinction between "smooth" and "striated" spaces. Rhizomatic structures are characteristic of the former, and critics such as Steve Shaviro have claimed that "World Wide Web browsers turn the Internet into what Deleuze and Guattari call smooth or rhizomatic space: a space of 'acentered systems, finite networks of automata in which communication runs from any neighbor to any other, the stems or channels do not pre-exist, and all individuals are interchangeable, defined only by their state at a given moment'" (quoted in Nunes 65).

3. Weblogs and webrings created by individuals to link and annotate each other's personal pages do possess some of the features of rhizomatic rather than menu-driven types of racial identification. These would seem to

allow the user a more free-form medium for defining her racial identities on the web rather than constraining them within a series of clickable, limited choices. More research remains to be done on the ways that racial identity is constructed by these intertextual links between websites.

4. Excite's website has changed since the time this chapter was written. Websites change their content frequently, and when I lasted checked in 2000, the list of identity choices under the *racial* search path had changed slightly. For example, Military and Veterans has been substituted for Virtual Worlds, and the Religion link has been omitted. Nonetheless, the same basic principle of design and hierarchical listing still obtains.

5. Women are also strikingly underrepresented in the field of software engineering, and recent research on this topic indicates an alarming trend toward even less gender equality in the field:

> According to the National Science Foundation, the number of bachelor degrees in computer science awarded to females was 40 percent in 1984, says Anita Borg, founding director of the Institute for Women in Technology (IWT) and a member of the research staff at Xerox's Palo Alto Research Center in California. That number has dropped to 27.5 percent, according to the U.S. Department of Education's most recent survey of 1996 graduates. (Radcliff n.p.)

6. This metaphor is literally true in the case of Disney's Go Network, which is linked to both Disney's website and Infoseek's portal: these three sites have multiple other linked corporate partners. Disney's media empire, like the merger of AOL and Time Warner, is an example of the ways in which older media have been forming alliances with Internet-oriented media, a move that casts even more doubt upon the ability of the Internet to produce content and form that is "new" and ideologically distinct from the mainstream.

7. The "one drop" rule, or the "folk belief that any admixture of African blood, no matter how remote, made one irrevocably black" (Stephens 28), was legally established in 1896 in *Plessy v. Ferguson*. Stephens rightly terms this the "one drop *ideology*," since its implications go far beyond the legal realm: "it is a racialized Puritanism taken to its logical extreme, in which the repression of the interracial and the repression of the sexual were deeply intertwined" (29).

8. Haraway defines *situated knowledge* as an "insistence" upon recognizing "contradictory moments and a wariness of their resolution, dialectically or otherwise" (111). In practice, this constitutes a revision of received cultural narratives produced by "histories of masculinist, racist, and colo-

nial dominations" (111) in such a way as to avoid replacing them with oppressive new ways of essentializing people. For example, a "situated" feminism or multiculturalism would carefully avoid demonizing all men or white people in a knee-jerk sort of way, and would instead examine the local, specific, and particular conditions of gender and race in a given moment or situation.

9. The "Only a Black Woman" list, which was passed on to me by an African American colleague, ends with the following exhortation: "If you are BLACK in origin please do not delete . . . pass it on to 10 good friends of yours . . . Let the Black people come together. . . ." In this way, the list overtly encourages recipients to extend the rhizomatic network of racial identity e-mail links between users. Unlike the JA list, however, it stresses the status of this text as a way for black people to "come together" online, without particularly calling into question what constitutes a black person.

CONCLUSION: KEEPING IT (VIRTUALLY) REAL

1. Both hip-hop and the Internet have relatively long histories prior to the mid-1990s. Indeed, these histories possess some striking parallels: while "during the late 1970's and early 1980's, the market for hip-hop was still based inside New York's black and Hispanic communities" (Rose 40), during this same period the majority of Internet users were based inside the overwhelmingly white, male, middle-class communities of computer hobbyists and engineers. Thus, both hip-hop and the Internet were raced activities that began to cross over into the mainstream at about the same time (though, particularly in the case of the Internet, that crossing over has still yet to transcend racial boundaries—see Hoffman and Novak on the digital divide.) I owe a considerable debt to Kim Hester-Williams for her insights and knowledge regarding the history of hip-hop.

2. Foster's own essay "'The Souls of Cyber-Folk'" is a notable exception to this rule, since it does engage the critical issues surrounding race and cyberculture. In fact, in this essay he speculates that the reason gender rather than race has been the focus of critical writing on cyberculture is that "one dominant tendency in both critical and popular narratives of cyberspace and [virtual reality] has been to emphasize subversive performativity, and therefore to emphasize gender, at the expense of attention to the racial implications of these new technologies" (139).

3. Though Mosaic, a program that "read" Web pages, but in a text-only environment, did exist and was used prior to 1995, it was only after the acceptance of Netscape as an industry standard that the web became a popular medium.

4. The burden of racial representativity borne by academics of color can take subtle and insidious forms. I have heard numerous narratives about and by newly hired Asian American, African American, and Latino scholars in the humanities who were hired for positions in film studies or English that did not require or mention training in ethnic studies, yet who were assigned courses in minority literatures in addition to teaching loads in their fields of specialization.

5. As Emily Toth notes in *Ms. Mentor's Impeccable Advice for Women in Academia*, many of these conditions obtain for female faculty as well, who, for reasons having to do with gender stereotyping, are also expected to spend more time "nurturing" and acting as surrogate mothers to their students. See also Anne duCille's *Skin Trade* on women of color in academe.

WORKS CITED

INTRODUCTION

Brooks, David. "The Day After." *New York Times Magazine* May 13, 2001:28.

Du Bois, W. E. B. *The Souls of Black Folk.* New York: Dover, 1903.

Gleick, James. *Faster: The Acceleration of Just about Everything.* New York: Vintage, 2000.

Harper, Phillip Brian. *Framing the Margins: The Social Logic of Postmodern Culture.* Oxford: Oxford University Press, 1994.

Heilemann, John. "Andy Grove's Rational Exuberance." *Wired* June 2001:137–47.

Kaplan, Caren. *Questions of Travel: Postmodern Discourses of Displacement.* Durham, NC: Duke University Press, 1996.

Punday, Daniel. "The Narrative Construction of Cyberspace: Reading *Neuromancer,* Reading Cyberspace Debates." *College English* 63.2 (November 2000):194–213.

Silver, David. "Margins in the Wires: Looking for Race, Gender, and Sexuality in the Blacksburg Electronic Village." In *Race in Cyberspace.* Ed. Beth Kolko, Lisa Nakamura, and Gilbert B. Rodman. New York: Routledge, 2000.

CHAPTER 1: CYBERTYPING AND THE WORK OF RACE IN THE AGE OF DIGITAL REPRODUCTION

Aarseth, Espen. "The Field of Humanistic Informatics and its Relation to the Humanities." Online at http://www.hf.uib.no/hi/espen/HI.html.

Austen, Ian. "Studies Reveal a Rush of Older Women to the Web." *New York Times,* June 29, 2000:D7.

Bukatman, Scott. *Terminal Identity: The Virtual Subject in Postmodern Fiction.* Durham, NC: Duke University Press, 1998.

Chow, Rey. *Writing Diaspora: Tactics of Intervention in Contemporary Cultural Studies.* Bloomington: Indiana University Press, 1993.

Christian, Barbara. "The Race for Theory." *Feminist Literary Theory: A Reader.* Ed. Mary Eagleton. London: Blackwell, 1986.

Davis, Mike. *Magical Urbanism: Latinos Reinvent the U.S. Big City.* London: Verso, 2000.

Fallows, James. "The Invisible Poor." *New York Times Magazine*, March 19, 2000, 8–78, 95, 111–12.

Gajjala, Radhika. "Transnational Digital Subjects: Constructs of Identity and Ignorance in a Digital Economy." Paper presented at the Conference on Cultural Diversity in Cyberspace, College Park, MD, May 2000.

Gomez-Peña, Guillermo. *Dangerous Border Crossers*. London and New York: Routledge, 2000.

Gonzalez, Jennifer. "The Appended Subject: Race and Identity as Digital Assemblage." *Race in Cyberspace*. Ed. Beth Kolko, Lisa Nakamura, and Gilbert B. Rodman. New York: Routledge, 2000.

Halberstam, Judith, and Ira Livingston, eds. *Posthuman Bodies*. Bloomington: Indiana University Press, 1995.

Hamilton, Martha. "Web Retailer Kozmo Accused of Redlining: Exclusion of D.C. Minority Areas Cited." *Washington Post*, April 14, 2000. Online at http://www.washingtonpost.com/wp-dyn/articles/A9719-2000Apr13.html.

Haraway, Donna. *Simians, Cyborgs, and Women: The Reinvention of Nature*. New York: Routledge, 1991.

Hartouni, Valerie. "Containing Women: Reproductive Discourse in the 1980s." *Technoculture*. Ed. Constance Penley and Andrew Ross. Minneapolis: University of Minnesota Press, 1991.

Hayles, N. Katherine. *How We Became Posthuman*. Chicago: U of Chicago P, 1999.

hooks, bell. *Black Looks: Race and Representation*. Boston: South End Press, 1992.

Katz, Frances. "Racial-Bias Suit Filed Against Online Delivery Service Kozmo.com." *KRTBN Knight-Ridder Tribune Business News: The Atlanta Journal and Constitution*, April 14, 2000.

Kraut, Robert and Vicki Lundmark. "Internet Paradox: A Social Technology That Reduces Social Involvement and Psychological Well-Being?" *American Psychologist*, 53.9 (1998):1017–31.

Kumar, Amitava. "Temporary Access: the Indian H1-B Visa Worker in the United States." *Technicolor: Race, Technology, and Everyday Life*. Ed. Alondra Nelson and Thuy Linh N. Tu with Alicia Headlam Hines. New York: New York University Press, 2001.

Lewis, Michael. "The Search Engine." *New York Times Magazine*, October 10, 1999, 77–83+.

Lorde, Audre. "The Master's Tools Will Never Dismantle the Master's House." *This Bridge Called My Back: Writing by Radical Women of Color*. Eds. Cherríe Moraga and Gloria Anzaldúa. New York: Kitchen Table Press, 1981.

Manovich, Lev. *The Language of New Media*. Cambridge, MA: MIT, 2001.

Netnoir.com Newsletter. Online mailing list.

Prakash, Snigdha. *All Things Considered*. National Public Radio. May 2, 2000. http://search.npr.org/cf/cmn/cmpd01fm.cfm?PrgDate=05% 2F02%2F2000&PrgID=2.

Prashad, Vijay. *The Karma of Brown Folk*. Minneapolis: University of Minnesota Press, 2000.

Sardar, Ziauddin. "Alt.Civilizations.FAQ: Cyberspace as the Darker Side of the West." *The Cybercultures Reader*. Ed. David Bell and Barbara Kennedy. New York: Routledge, 2000.

Spivak, Gayatri Chakravorty. *In Other Worlds: Essays in Cultural Politics*. New York: Routledge, 1988.

Stephensen, Neal. *The Diamond Age*. New York: Bantam, 1995.

Stewart, Susan. *On Longing: Narratives of the Miniature, the Gigantic, the Souvenir, the Collection*. Durham, NC: Duke University Press, 1993.

Stone, Allucquère Rosanne. *The War of Desire and Technology*. Cambridge, MA: MIT Press, 1995.

Tal, Kalí. "The Unbearable Whiteness of Being: African American Critical Theory and Cyberculture." Online at http://www.kalital.com/Text/ Writing/Whitenes.html.

Turkle, Sherry. *Life on the Screen: Identity in the Age of the Internet*. New York: Simon and Schuster, 1995.

CHAPTER 2: HEAD-HUNTING ON THE INTERNET

Aker, Sharon. *Macintosh Bible*. 3rd ed. Berkeley: Goldstein and Blair, 1991.

Bell, David, and Barbara M. Kennedy, eds. *The Cybercultures Reader*. New York: Routledge, 2000.

Butler, Judith. *Bodies That Matter: On the Discursive Limits of "Sex."* New York: Routledge, 1993.

Chesher, Chris. "Colonizing Virtual Reality: Construction of the Discourse of Virtual Reality, 1984–1992." *Cultronix* 1.1 (summer 1994).

Cherny, Lynn. *Conversation and Community: Discourse in a Social MUD*. Cambridge: Cambridge University Press, 1999.

Dibbell, Julian. *My Tiny Life*. New York: Owl Books, 1999.

————. "A Rape in Cyberspace" online at http://www.humanities.uci. edu/mposter/syllabi/readings/rape.html.

Elmer-Dewitt, Philip. "Battle for the Soul of the Internet." *Time*. July, 25 1994: 50.

Foster, Thomas. "'The Souls of Cyber-Folk': Performativity, Virtual Embodiment, and Racial Histories." *Cyberspace Textuality: Computer Technology and Literary Theory.* Ed. Marie-Laure Ryan. Bloomington: Indiana University Press, 1999. 137–63.

Gendron, Bernard. *Technology and the Human Condition.* New York: St. Martin's, 1977.

Haraway, Donna. *Simians, Cyborgs, and Women.* New York: Routledge, 1991.

Kingston, Maxine Hong. *The Woman Warrior.* New York: Knopf, 1977.

Kolbert, Elizabeth. "Pimps and Dragons (Dept. of Gaming)." *New Yorker,* May 28, 2001: 88–98.

MacCannell, Dean. *The Tourist: A New Theory of the Leisure Class.* New York: Schocken, 1989.

Nguyen, Mimi. "Tales of an Asiatic Geek Girl: *Slant* from Paper to Pixels." *Technicolor: Race, Technology, and Everday Life.* Ed. Alondra Nelson and Thuy Linh N. Tu with Alicia Headlam Hines. New York: New York University Press, 2001.

Ow, Jeff. "The Revenge of the Yellow-Faced Cyborg: The Rape of Digital Geishas and the Colonization of Cyber-Coolies in 3D Realms' Shadow Warrior." *Race in Cyberspace.* Ed. Beth Kolko, Lisa Nakamura, and Gilbert Rodman. London and New York: Routledge, 2000. 51–68.

Penley, Constance, and Andrew Ross. *Technoculture.* Minneapolis: University of Minnesota Press, 1991.

Rheingold, Howard. *The Virtual Community.* New York: HarperPerennial, 1993.

Ritzer, George, and Allan Liska. "'McDisneyization' and 'Post-Tourism': Complementary Perspectives on Contemporary Tourism." *Touring Cultures: Transformations of Travel and Theory.* Ed. Chris Rojek and John Urry. New York and London: Routledge, 1997.

Stone, Allucquère Rosanne. "Will the Real Body Please Stand Up? Boundary Stories about Virtual Cultures." *Cyberspace: First Steps.* Ed. Michael Benedikt. Cambridge, MA: MIT Press, 1994.

Said, Edward. Introduction. *Kim,* by Rudyard Kipling. New York: Penguin, 1987.

Silverman, Kaja. "Back to the Future." *Alien Zone.* Ed. Annette Kuhn. London: Verso, 1990.

Smith, Marc A., and Peter Kollock, eds. *Communities in Cyberspace.* New York: Routledge, 1999.

Trinh T. Minh-ha. *Woman, Native, Other: Writing Postcoloniality and Feminism.* Bloomington: Indiana University Press, 1989.

CHAPTER 3: RACE IN THE CONSTRUCT AND THE CONSTRUCTION OF RACE

Anthony, Ted. "At the Movies: The Matrix," *Entertainment News*, March 30, 1999, online at http://www.laprensa-sandiego.org/archieve/april02/movies.htm.

Blade Runner. Dir. Ridley Scott. Warner Bros., 1982.

Brande, David. "The Business of Cyberpunk: Symbolic Economy and Ideology in William Gibson." *configurations* (Fall 1994):509–36.

Bukatman, Scott. *Terminal Identity: The Virtual Subject in Postmodern Science Fiction*. Durham, NC: Duke University Press, 1993.

Carroll, Lewis. *The Lewis Carroll Book*. New York: Tudor, 1939.

Cherny, Lynn. and Elizabeth Reba Weise, eds. *Wired Women: Gender and New Reality in Cyberspace*. Seattle: Seal Press, 1996.

Crane, David. "In Medias Race: Filmic Representation, Networked Communication, and Racial Intermediation." *Race in Cyberspace*. Ed. Beth E. Kolko, Lisa Nakamura, and Gilbert B. Rodman. New York: Routledge, 2000.

Croal, N'Gai. "Maximizing the Matrix." *Newsweek*, April 19, 1999: 64.

Delany, Samuel. "Racism and Science Fiction." *Dark Matter: A Century of Speculative Fiction from the African Diaspora*. Ed. Sheree R. Thomas. New York: Warner Books, 2000.

DeVries, Hilary. "Hot Pinkett." *W*, May 2001: 121–24.

Gibson, William. "Modern Boys and Mobile Girls." *Guardian*, April 1, 2001. Online at http://books.guardian.co.uk/departments/sciencefiction/story/0,6000,466421,00.html.

————. *Neuromancer*. New York: Ace, 1984.

Foster, Thomas. "'Trapped by the Body?' Telepresence Technologies and Transgendered Performance in Feminist and Lesbian Rewritings of Cyberpunk Fiction." *Modern Fiction Studies* 43.3 (Fall 1997): 708–42.

Hoffman, Donna, and Thomas P. Novak, "Bridging the Digital Divide: The Impact of Race on Computer Access and Internet Use." Project 2000, Vanderbilt University, 29 January 1999. Online at http://www2000.ogsm.vanderbilt.edu/papers/race/science/html.

Holmes, Steven A. "The Confusion Over Who We Are." *New York Times*, Sunday, June 3, 2001: sec. 4, pp. 1, 5.

Lipsitz, George. *The Possessive Investment in Whiteness: How White People Profit from Identity Politics*. Philadelphia: Temple University Press, 1998.

The Matrix. Dir. Andy and Larry Wachowski. Warner Bros., 1999.

Mitchell, Elvis. "Character Assassination." "Fashions of the Times" special supplement, *New York Times*. Spring, 2000: part 2, 52.

Morrison, Toni. *Playing in the Dark*. New York: Vintage, 1992.

Niu, Greta Ai-Yu. "Techno-Orientalism, Cyborgology and Asian American Studies." Paper presented at the Discipline and Deviance: Genders, Technologies, Machines Conference, Duke University, October 1998.

Porush, David. "Hacking the Brainstem: Postmodern Metaphysics and Stephenson's *Snow Crash*." *Virtual Realities and Their Discontents*. Ed. Robert Markley. Baltimore: Johns Hopkins University Press, 1996.

Stephenson, Neal. *The Diamond Age*. New York: Bantam, 1995.

———. *Snow Crash*. New York: Bantam Spectra, 1992.

Sterling, Bruce. "Bruce Sterling: Cyberpunk in the Nineties." *Interzone* 48 (June 1, 1991): 39–41.

Stone, Allucquère Rosanne. *The War of Desire and Technology*. Cambridge, MA: MIT Press, 1995.

Strange Days. Dir. Kathryn Bigelow. TriMark, 1995.

Turkle, Sherry. *Life on the Screen*. New York: Simon and Schuster, 1995.

CHAPTER 4: "WHERE DO YOU WANT TO GO TODAY?"

Hollinger, David. *Postethnic America: Beyond Multiculturalism*. New York: Basic Books, 1995.

Kaplan, Caren. *Questions of Travel: Postmodern Discourses of Displacement*. Durham, NC: Duke University Press, 1996.

MacCannell, Dean. *The Tourist: A New Theory of the Leisure Class*. New York: Schocken, 1989.

McLuhan, Marshall. *Understanding Media: The Extensions of Man*. Cambridge, MA: MIT Press, 1994.

Rushdie, Salman. "Damme, This is the Oriental Scene for You!" *New Yorker*. June 23 and 30, 1997: 50–61.

Trinh T. Minh-ha. *Woman, Native, Other: Writing Postcoloniality and Feminism*. Bloomington: Indiana University Press, 1989.

Wise, John Macgregor. "The Virtual Community: Politics and Affect in Cyberspace." Paper presented at the American Studies Association Conference, Washington DC, October 1997.

CHAPTER 5: MENU-DRIVEN IDENTITIES

Anzaldúa, Gloria. *Borderlands/La Frontera*. San Francisco: Aunt Lute Books, 1987.

Bakhtin, Mikhail. *The Dialogic Imagination*. Austin: University of Texas Press, 1981.

Crane, David. "In Medias Race: Filmic Representation, Networked Communication, and Racial Intermediation." *Race in Cyberspace*. Ed. Beth E. Kolko, Lisa Nakamura, and Gilbert Rodman. New York: Routledge. 2000.

Hoffman, Donna, and Thomas P. Novak. "Bridging the Digital Divide: The Impact of Race on Computer Access and Internet Use." Project 2000, Vanderbilt University, January 29, 1999. Online at http://www.2000.ogsm.vanderbilt.edu/papers/race/science/html.

Lowe, Lisa. *Immigrant Acts: On Asian American Cultural Politics*. Durham, NC: Duke University Press, 1996.

McLaine, Steven. "Ethnic Online Communities: Between Profit and Purpose." Paper presented at the Cyberculture(s): Performance, Pedagogy and Politics in Online Spaces Conference, University of Maryland, April 2001.

Nunes, Mark. "Virtual Topographies: Smooth and Striated Cyberspace." *Cyberspace Textuality: Computer Technology and Literary Theory*. Ed. Marie-Laure Ryan. Bloomington: Indiana University Press, 1999.

Poster, Mark. *The Second Media Age*. Cambridge: Polity Press, 1995.

Radcliff, Deborah. "Biz Careers: Champions of Women in Technology." *Computer World*, April 18, 1999. Online at http://www.computerworld.com/home/features.nsf/all/990118women.

Stephens, Gregory. *On Racial Frontiers: the New Culture of Frederick Douglass, Ralph Ellison, and Bob Marley*. Cambridge: Cambridge University Press, 1999.

Sterne, Jonathan. "The Computer Race Meets Computer Classes: How Computers in Schools Helped Shape the Racial Topography of the Internet." *Race in Cyberspace*. Ed. Beth E. Kolko, Lisa Nakamura, and Gilbert B. Rodman. New York: Routledge, 2000.

Stone, Allucquère Rosanne. "Will the Real Body Please Stand Up? Boundary Stories about Visual Cultures." *Cyberspace: First Steps*. Ed. Michael Benedict. Cambridge. MA: MIT Press, 1994.

Turkle, Sherry. *Life on the Screen: Identity in the Age of the Internet*. New York: Touchstone, 1997.

Zickmund, Susan. "Approaching the Radical Other: The Discursive Culture of Cyberhate." *The Cybercultures Reader*. Ed. David Bell and Barbara Kennedy. London: Routledge. 2000. 237–253.

CONLCUSION: KEEPING IT (VIRTUALLY) REAL

Austen, Ian. "Studies Reveal a Rush of Older Women to the Web." *New York Times*, June 29, 2000: D7.

Bow, Leslie. "Erasure and Representation: Asian American Women in the Academy." *Profession 1997*. New York: Modern Language Associaton of America, 1997. 215–221.

duCille, Ann. *Skin Trade*. Cambridge, MA: Harvard University Press, 1996.

Foster, Thomas. "'The Souls of Cyber-Folk: Performativity, Virtual Embodiment, and Racial Histories." *Cyberspace Textuality: Computer Technology and Literary Theory*. Ed. Marie-Laure Ryan. Bloomington: Indiana University Press, 1999.

Harper, Phillip Brian. *Framing the Margins: The Social Logic of Postmodern Culture*. Oxford: Oxford University Press, 1994.

Jones, Steven G., ed. *Cybersociety 2.0*. Thousand Oaks, CA: Sage Publications, 1998.

Roberts, Sam. "Writing about Race (And Trying to Talk about It)." *New York Times Magazine*, July 16, 2000: 16–22.

Rose, Tricia. *Black Noise : Rap Music and Black Culture in Contemporary America*. Wesleyan University Press, 1994.

Silver, David, ed. *The Resource Center for Cyberculture Studies*. Department of Communication, the University of Washington. http://www.com.washington.edu/rccs/.

Tal, Kalí. "The Unbearable Whiteness of Being: African American Critical Theory and Cyberculture." http://www.kalital.com/Text/Writing/Whitenes.html.

United States Department of Education. *Digest of Educational Statistics*. 1999. NCES. Online at http://www.nces.ed.gov/.

INDEX

Lightning Source UK Ltd.
Milton Keynes UK
UKOW041106051012

200069UK00006B/27/P